SOCIAL ISSUES
FIRSTHAND

Learning Disabilities

Other Books in the Social Issues Firsthand Series:

SOCIAL ISSUES
FIRSTHAND

Learning Disabilities

Sharon Gunton, Book Editor

GREENHAVEN PRESS
A part of Gale, Cengage Learning

GALE
CENGAGE Learning

Detroit • New York • San Francisco • New Haven, Conn • Waterville, Maine • London

Christine Nasso, *Publisher*
Elizabeth Des Chenes, *Managing Editor*

© 2008 Greenhaven Press, a part of Gale, Cengage Learning.

For more information, contact:
Greenhaven Press
27500 Drake Rd.
Farmington Hills, MI 48331-3535
Or you can visit our Internet site at gale.cengage.com

ISBN-13: 978-0-7377-3840-7 (hardcover)
ISBN-10: 0-7377-3840-5 (hardcover)

Library of Congress Control Number: 2007933683

Printed in the United States of America
2 3 4 5 6 7 12 11 10 09 08

Contents

Foreword

S ocial issues are often viewed in abstract terms. Pressing challenges such as poverty, homelessness, and addiction are viewed as problems to be defined and solved. Politicians, social scientists, and other experts engage in debates about the extent of the problems, their causes, and how best to remedy them. Often overlooked in these discussions is the human dimension of the issue. Behind every policy debate over poverty, homelessness, and substance abuse, for example, are real people struggling to make ends meet, to survive life on the streets, and to overcome addiction to drugs and alcohol. Their stories are ubiquitous and compelling. They are the stories of everyday people—perhaps your own family members or friends—and yet they rarely influence the debates taking place in state capitols, the national Congress, or the courts.

The disparity between the public debate and private experience of social issues is well illustrated by looking at the topic of poverty. Each year the U.S. Census Bureau establishes a poverty threshold. A household with an income below the threshold is defined as poor, while a household with an income above the threshold is considered able to live on a basic subsistence level. For example, in 2003 a family of two was considered poor if its income was less than $12,015; a family of four was defined as poor if its income was less than $18,810. Based on this system, the bureau estimates that 35.9 million Americans (12.5 percent of the population) lived below the poverty line in 2003, including 12.9 million children below the age of eighteen.

Commentators disagree about what these statistics mean. Social activists insist that the huge number of officially poor Americans translates into human suffering. Even many families that have incomes above the threshold, they maintain, are likely to be struggling to get by. Other commentators insist that the statistics exaggerate the problem of poverty in the United States. Compared to people in developing countries, they point out, most so-called poor families have a high quality of life. As stated by journalist Fidelis Iyebote, "Cars are owned by 70 percent of 'poor' households. . . . Color televisions belong to 97 percent of the 'poor' [and] videocassette recorders belong to nearly 75 percent. . . . Sixty-four percent have microwave ovens, half own a stereo system, and over a quarter possess an automatic dishwasher."

However, this debate over the poverty threshold and what it means is likely irrelevant to a person living in poverty. Simply put, poor people do not need the government to tell them whether they are poor. They can see it in the stack of bills they cannot pay. They are aware of it when they are forced to choose between paying rent or buying food for their children. They become painfully conscious of it when they lose their homes and are forced to live in their cars or on the streets. Indeed, the written stories of poor people define the meaning of poverty more vividly than a government bureaucracy could ever hope to. Narratives composed by the poor describe losing jobs due to injury or mental illness, depict horrific tales of childhood abuse and spousal violence, recount the loss of friends and family members. They evoke the slipping away of social supports and government assistance, the descent into substance abuse and addiction, the harsh realities of life on the streets. These are the perspectives on poverty that are too often omitted from discussions over the extent of the problem and how to solve it.

Greenhaven Press's Social Issues Firsthand series provides a forum for the often-overlooked human perspectives on society's most divisive topics of debate. Each volume focuses on one social issue and presents a collection of ten to sixteen narratives by those who have had personal involvement with the topic. Extra care has been taken to include a diverse range of perspectives. For example, in the volume on adoption, readers will find the stories of birth parents who have made an adoption plan, adoptive parents, and adoptees themselves. After exposure to these varied points of view, the reader will have a clearer understanding that adoption is an intense, emotional experience full of joyous highs and painful lows for all concerned.

The debate surrounding embryonic stem cell research illustrates the moral and ethical pressure that the public brings to bear on the scientific community. However, while nonexperts often criticize scientists for not considering the potential negative impact of their work, ironically the public's reaction against such discoveries can produce harmful results as well. For example, although the outcry against embryonic stem cell research in the United States has resulted in fewer embryos being destroyed, those with Parkinson's, such as actor Michael J. Fox, have argued that prohibiting the development of new stem cell lines ultimately will prevent a timely cure for the disease that is killing Fox and thousands of others.

Each book in the series contains several features that enhance its usefulness, including an in-depth introduction, an annotated table of contents, bibliographies for further research, a list of organizations to contact, and a thorough index. These elements—combined with the poignant voices of people touched by tragedy and triumph—make the Social Issues Firsthand series a valuable resource for research on today's topics of political discussion.

On April 6, 1963, a conference was held in Chicago so that experts might share their opinions about the treatment and diagnosis of certain learning difficulties in children of apparently normal, or above normal, intelligence. The conference was named "Exploration into the Problems of the Perceptually Handicapped Child," but from the title of a paper delivered by Dr. Samuel Kirk, the term "learning disability" was adopted. At present, six main types of learning disorders are generally cited and roughly defined as:

dysgraphia—difficulty with spelling, handwriting, and expressing thoughts in writing

dyscalculia—difficulty with math and quantitative skills, time, and direction

dyslexia—difficulty with reading and writing

dysparaxia—difficulty with planning and completing fine motor tasks

nonverbal learning disabilities (or NLD)—difficulty with body language, communication skills, spatial perception, fine motor skills, and abstract reasoning

attention deficit disorder and attention deficit hyperactive disorder (or ADD and ADHD)—difficulty with concentration and completion of tasks, often coupled with a tendency toward impulsivity and, in ADHD, hyperactivity.

During the 1960s, learning disabilities were the subject of much writing, research, and discussion. Because the symptoms of learning difficulties were often revealed and studied in the classroom, they were given a strictly academic focus and considered to have ramifications in terms of learning and testing only.

Social Challenges for the Learning Disabled

But, as detailed by Bernice Y.L. Wong in *The ABCs of Learning Disabilities*, research done in the 1970s scrutinized the social and psychological aspects of learning differences. Even then, the problems that most learning disabled people seemed to have in relationships were thought to be simply a matter of low self-esteem, brought on by years of struggle, and sometimes failure, in the learning environment.

However, many researchers believed that something else was going on. They felt that the same cluster of challenges found in academic settings were present in social situations and these challenges were especially problematic for those with learning disabilities. People with learning difficulties often misinterpret body language, or don't notice it at all. And because social situations include information that is often abstract and in constant flux, it can be very difficult for learning disabled people to stay in touch with these changes. Subtle and complex social interactions are particularly tricky. Negotiation or persuasion is often needed in a social situation or a discussion. As noted on the Web site of the Learning Disabilities Association of Canada, learning difficulties impact one's ability to "pay attention, comprehend, conceptualize, visualize, communicate, be organized, follow conversations, interpret body language, etc." Experts felt these obstacles would complicate all three major areas of social interaction: input, processing, and output. In other words, not only does a learning disabled person find it hard to understand what others are saying or showing through gestures and body language, but they have trouble analyzing this information and coming to resolutions concerning appropriate solutions. In addition, they have a hard time composing and communicating their own thoughts and desires.

These challenges often begin in the school years, as outlined by Richard Lavoie, an expert in special education who has studied social competence. Lavoie writes eloquently on his

Web site about the subject of how learning disabled students interact with others: "Social skills are a collection of isolated and discrete learned behaviors. Social competence refers to the smooth sequential use of these skills in an effort to establish an ongoing social interaction. There are two schools of thought related to the nature and causes of social incompetence [in learning disabled people]. Proponents of the first hypothesis argue that social skill deficits are the result of the same neurological dysfunctions that cause academic problems. The second hypothesis holds that the social disabilities are caused by the child's chronic school failure and the rejection that often results. These researchers feel that the child has been unable to practice these social skills because of this isolation." Lavoie goes on to say that the reason for social incompetence is far less important than its effect on the person's life. He and other experts believe that the effects of social problems in the school years often lead to problems with relationships in adulthood.

Strategies for Improved Relationships

It is common for learning disabled people to flounder in relationships. However, experts seem to agree that there are many methods that can be used by learning disabled adults (and children, to some extent) to improve their relationships with others. One method is to recognize that everyone's relationships require constant work; the learning disabled are not alone in their struggle to perfect their relationships with others. Experts also advise that the learning disabled be as self-reliant as possible. Learning disabled people are often prone to welcome the help of providers, then become resentful and feel they are being treated like children. Most of all, experts advise communication. They tell learning disabled people to work to understand what they need at various times and make those needs known in very concrete terms. Ask for a list or memo, for example. Giving and getting feedback on a regular basis is crucial.

A 1981 study found that learning disabled children, when told they would be getting a visit from a TV personality who would ask them questions and give them gifts, were equally able to ingratiate themselves to their visitor as other children in the study. The conclusion that, when motivated, learning disabled people are capable of using socially acceptable and socially persuasive behaviors on par with anyone else. Proper motivation seems to be the key, according to this study which is explained fully in Bernice Y.L. Wong's book *The ABCs of Learning Disabilities*. And practice seems to be essential as well. In today's wired environment, learning disabled people may resort to the computer to connect with others in a comfortable, nonthreatening environment, but this cuts them off from vital face-to-face interaction and the chance to practice and perfect their personal social skills.

Success Stories

Needless to say, not all learning disabled people find it difficult to relate to others. Some are very social and extremely popular; others have worked on their interpersonal skills and flourished socially. Many individuals with learning disabilities have acquired a large degree of success in challenging, dynamic fields. Some experts in the field of learning disabilities suspect that Thomas Edison, Leonardo da Vinci, Albert Einstein, and Winston Churchill and many other famous people probably had learning disabilities of some sort. And many productive, prominent people today have learning disabilities: actors Orlando Bloom, Patrick Dempsey, and Kiera Knightly; designer Tommy Hilfiger; athlete and football analyst Terry Bradshaw; entrepreneur Richard Branson; HP cofounder Bill Hewlett; environmental activist Erin Brockovich; and comedian Jay Leno, just to name a few. These people—and the individuals in this book—live lives full of struggles, setbacks, and triumphs, and they typify the many faces of learning disabilities. Many experts say that those with learning difficulties are a testament to the fact that there is no "one size fits all" approach to life and, as the varied life stories of learning disabled individuals show, there is also no "one size fits all" description of a person who has learning differences.

SOCIAL ISSUES
FIRSTHAND

CHAPTER 1

Living with Learning Disabilities

Find a Place Where You Excel

Samantha Abeel

Because of dyscalculia, Samantha Abeel has great difficulty with tasks like telling time, following directions, and handling monetary transactions. Undiagnosed and terribly frustrated, she became withdrawn and anxious by the time she was in middle school. Fortunately, her mother and one of her teachers appreciated her writing abilities and urged her to write poems inspired by the paintings of Charles R. Murphy, a well-known artist and family friend. In the following excerpt from her book, Reach for the Moon, *Abeel shares her story and offers advice for others with learning disabilities. It is followed by a poem she wrote describing herself and alluding to her learning differences, titled "Self Portrait."*

Samantha's Story

A TREE that stands in the moonlight reflects the light, yet also casts a shadow. People are the same. They have gifts that let them shine, yet they also have disabilities, shadows that obscure the light. When I started this project in the seventh grade, I had trouble telling time, counting money, remembering even the simplest of addition and subtraction problems. Yet no matter how hard it was to stay afloat in this ocean of troubles, there was something inside of me, something that became my life preserver—and that was writing.

SEVENTH GRADE was a horrible year. I hated school. Every night I would come home and kiss the floor and revel that I had made it through one more day without totally messing up, or if I had, at least I was still alive. Then I would remember that I had to go back the next day and brave through all the same trials. With that thought, the tears and panic attacks grew. Yet one hour of my day was a refuge. Here, there weren't any concepts with numbers, measurements, algebra, or failure. It was my seventh-grade writing class. I had begun to experiment with creative writing in sixth grade, but in seventh grade I discovered how much writing was a part of me and I was a part of it.

TO BUILD on this, my mother asked Mrs. Williams, who was my English teacher, if she would work with me by giving me writing assignments and critiquing them as a way of focusing on what was right with me and not on what was wrong. Charles Murphy, a family friend, lent us slides and pictures of his beautiful watercolors. I began to write using his images as inspiration. I discovered that by crawling inside and becoming what I wrote, it made my writing and ideas more powerful.

IN EIGHTH GRADE I was finally recognized as learning disabled. I was taken from my seventh grade algebra class, where I was totally lost and placed in a special education resource classroom. Special education changed my life. It was the best thing that ever happened to me. I could raise my hand in that class, even when being taught the most elementary concepts, and say, "I don't get it." It was the most wonderful feeling in the world. Eighth grade was my best year at the junior high. It is an illusion that students in special education have no abilities. Special education just means that you learn differently. I am so thankful for specially trained teachers who have been able to help me and many other kids like me.

IF YOU STRUGGLE with a disability, the first thing you need to do is find something that you are good at, whether it's singing or skate boarding, an interest in science or acting, even just being good with people. Then do something with that. If you are good with people, then volunteer at a nursing home or at a day care center; if you love skate boarding, work toward a competition. If it's singing, join a school choir. Even

19

if you can't read music (like me) or read a script, you can always find ways of coping and compensating.

NEVER LET your disability stop you from doing what you are good at or want to do. I have trouble spelling and I'm horrible at grammar, but I was lucky enough to have teachers who graded me on the content of what I had to say instead of how bad my spelling and punctuation were. I was able to use a computer to compensate.

REMEMBER that if you have trouble in school, it might not be because you don't fit the school, it might be because the school doesn't fit you. Be an advocate for yourself. Keep trying. You may not fit in now, but whether you're seven or seventy, one day you will find a place where you excel.

AT THE BEGINNING of ninth grade we realized that what had started out as an art/poetry project had grown into something more. Because getting the right teachers and having the right educational placement made such a difference in my life, we realized it was a message we wanted to share. LD [the acronym for learning disabilities] does not mean "lazy and dumb." It just means you have another way of looking at the world. I hope through my writing and what we have all contributed to this book to remind people that if you're standing in the shadow of the tree, you may need to walk to the other side to see the light it reflects. They are both part of the same tree; both need to be recognized and understood. This is my reflection of the light.

Welcome to my book.—Samantha Abeel

"Self Portrait"

To show you who I am

I crawled inside a tree, became its
roots, bark and leaves,

listened to its whispers in the wind.

When fall came and painted the
leaves red and gold

I wanted to shake them across your
lawn
to transform the grass into a quilt,
a gift spread at your feet,
but their numbers eluded me,
so I turned a piece of paper into
my soul
to send to you so that you might
see
how easily it can be crumpled and
flattened out again.
I wanted you to see my resilience,
but I wasn't sure how to arrange
the numbers in your address,
so I danced with the Indians in the
forest
and collected the feathers that fell
from the eagle's wings,
each one a wish for my future,
but I lost track of their numbers,
gathered too many,
and was unable to carry them
home
so I reaped the wind with my hair,
relived its journey through my
senses, and
felt its whispered loneliness, like
lakes in winter,
but it was too far and you could
not follow me.
Now I've written out their shadows
like the wind collects its secrets
to whisper into receptive ears, and
I
will leave them at your doorstep,

a reminder of what others cannot
see,
a reminder of what I can and cannot be.

When Discovery Comes in Adulthood

Henry Winkler

Sometimes awareness that you have a learning disability comes after many years of difficulty and confusion. It is common for adults to say that for decades they battled with conflicting feelings. They thought they were very bright, yet struggled constantly in school (often failing or dropping out), and just didn't know how to handle certain life situations. When their children are diagnosed with a learning disability, or they hear about learning disabilities from some other source, it is a true revelation; many say they understand themselves for the first time in their lives.

Actor Henry Winkler, best known for his role as Arthur Fonzarelli in the TV series Happy Days, *didn't realize he had a learning disability until he was an adult. When Winkler was in his early thirties, he was asked to narrate a film on learning disabilities in 1976, and as soon as he read the descriptions of dyslexia for the film, he instantly recognized his own symptoms. Since then he has become a spokesman on the subject and has penned a series of humorous books for young readers, featuring learning disabled protagonist Hank Zipzer.*

The following is an excerpt from a speech Winkler gave in 1988 about dyslexia.

So as I'm reading the narration into a tape recorder, it started to dawn on me. I'm not lazy. I'm not stupid. I'm dyslexic . . .

Until recently, my reach was always beyond my grasp. I had dreams. . . . I was not the best student in the world, and my parents were strict. So I would dream a lot about grasp-

Henry Winkler,. "A Man's Reach Should Exceed His Grasp," *Perspectives*, vol. 17, January 1989. Reproduced by permission.

ing, but I spent most of my time merely reaching. And it was difficult to fathom the fact that I could grasp.

I'm 42 years old, and I'm very proud to say that my self image is here! It's around my collarbone: for a long time it was around my ankles and I spent a lot of time pulling it up. That was at a time when I was known as lazy and not living up to my potential.

A Search for Answers

The idea going around in my head at that time was that I might be stupid. How could this be happening to me? My parents came from Germany; they learned English and several other languages, they could do their math in their heads. . . . How could I be stupid? I didn't want to be stupid, I wanted to be in the top ten percent of my class, not the bottom three.

The headmaster of my high school sent me to a psychiatrist because he wanted to know why I wasn't achieving. So the psychiatrist said to my parents, who took copious notes, "The boy has to learn to focus!" Hooray, the problem was solved, I knew what to do. I went to the stationery store and got myself some highlighters. . . . Blue and yellow. And I went home and I highlighted every word in the book. And it was still Greek to me! I didn't get it; alright, maybe I had brain damage.

And I didn't want to have brain damage but I tell you, the thought gave me comfort. And it gave me even greater comfort as keeping up with my class became harder and harder. I went to a private school in New York City, with a lot of guys who wore cordovan shoes, blue blazers, grey slacks, and a tie to school every day . . . they were going to Princeton. They wrote notes in the margins of the books they were reading for class . . . were they writing?

So do you know what I did? I took a glass of water and sprinkled drops of it on the page . . . so the book looked used. I never wrote anything in my book except my name . . . very neatly.

For me math is out of the question. When I got change, I trusted a lot. I had no idea how much was in my palm. Reading was slow because my eyes couldn't track, I would leave out words. And spelling was something other people could do. To this day the only way I survive is that I have a secretary in an office next to mine and I spend most of my time yelling, "How do you spell circle?"

The Answer Comes Unexpectedly

Somewhere inside me the thought kept gnawing at me that something was wrong; something about what the outside world was telling me was not connecting with what my inside world knew. Except that my inside knowledge kept me moving forward, because I wanted to be somebody. I was tired of being a dope!

And then this surface view of myself kept throwing self doubt the size of apartment buildings in front of me, so that getting to be "somebody" was a little slower than I wanted it to be.

Because of my character on *Happy Days* I was asked to narrate a film for students with learning disabilities in 1976. It was called *Everybody Has a Song*. Of course I wanted to help these poor kids with this problem! So as I'm reading the narration into a tape recorder, it started to dawn on me. I'm not lazy. I'm not stupid. *I'm dyslexic!!!* Who knew? Nobody knew when I was growing up.

So as an adult I'm standing here not understanding all the concepts of the Isosceles Triangle. . . . But, I learned to compensate. I learned to listen to my instincts, that if you will it, it is not a dream. If you are able to communicate your feelings, you too, can speak an international, very articulate language. I learned to problem solve. My friends would always have a social problem, and since I took most of my cues from the physical world around me, I was able to sit with them and tell them how they got into the problem, what it was doing to them, and how they could get out of trouble. I had no idea how I knew this stuff, but lots of times I was right and it felt very good that I was able to do something for them!

When I was growing up no one knew that dyslexia might have been caused by genetics. But the fact is a lot of you do know this now. Because you do, you understand the best teacher is not necessarily the one who deals with the most facts, but who effectively allows the student to come to grips with the best part of themselves.

Throughout history the same thoughts keep coming up. Thank God for our difficulties; because through them we find ourselves! And because of difficulties we find we are not alone. It gave me great comfort to hear how hard it is for other people to do the same things I can't.

I Say Learning Differences

Charlotte Farber

Charlotte Farber's mother is famous fashion designer Dana Buchman. After Charlotte was diagnosed with a learning disability as well as some problems with motor coordination, visual processing, and other neurological functioning, the family dealt with it as a loving, albeit fallible team. Buchman wrote the book A Special Education: One Family's Journey through the Maze of Learning Disabilities *about their struggles and successes. She donates proceeds from the book to the National Center for Learning Disabilities.*

Charlotte wrote the afterword to her mother's book, from which the following excerpt is taken. She relates how she has come to appreciate that she has many admirable attributes that are linked to her learning disability. She has found in herself a deep pool of compassion for others, great tenacity, artistic talent, and the ability to read backward. Although she acknowledges the discouraging and sometimes embarrassing limitations of her learning disability, she recognizes and appreciates her gifts and talents. Because of this, Farber has come to consider herself as someone with learning differences, not disabilities.

I say *learning differences* instead of *learning disabilities* because the word "disability" makes it seem like we're not capable of learning. But we are—we just need to have things taught to us differently because our brains are wired differently. Sometimes, though, I have to live with the "disability" label so that I can get special considerations, like untimed tests.

But I hate the word "disability." It makes some people think having LD [a learning disability] means you're not smart at all, or academically flawed. I've seen the reactions on some people's faces when I've told them about my differences. They look really confused and don't know what to say. Or they say dumb things, like, "So, does that mean you're stupid?" I mean, do I *look* stupid? I feel like telling them, "You would never know I was an LD kid if I didn't tell you."

Well, okay, if I'm totally honest, I can see why some people might think that, at times, like when they catch me going in the wrong direction or being completely disorganized. My locker in high school was a big mess, and when I'd open it, papers would fly out. It's what I called "the Charlotte tornado" when friends or teachers would try and help me with it.

So, yeah, there are things that my learning differences make difficult for me that most people take for granted. Like being able to measure with a ruler, which to me may as well be a blank stick because of my problems with math and numbers. Or knowing which basket to shoot the ball in during a basketball game. I once scored points for the other team because I have issues with spatial relations, and went the wrong way.

Being Honest Proves Effective

It's those sorts of things that make me feel humiliated in public, and make me want to hide and not try. I have been working on getting over that, and trying anyway. Part of that is getting comfortable with telling people I have LD, and asking for help when I need it. That would be a lot easier if LD wasn't this subject that no one talked about. I wish people talked about it more. It would seem less like a secret or a big deal. It's like sex—it's in the shhhhh box.

I have been having more and more positive experiences with telling people lately. In my last year of high school, I was at Barnes & Noble, looking for *The Great Train Robbery* for my English class. I had misplaced the school copy and had to replace it. I asked the woman at the information desk where I could find it. She looked it up in the computer, and then told me, "Look in the back, two aisles down." At least that was what I thought she said. So I went and looked. And I looked, and I looked. But my difficulties with directions and organization combined to make it really hard for me.

I could have just given up, and at one time, I would have. But on this day, I went back to the woman at the information desk. I kind of chuckled and said, "Um, I have problems with directions, and I was wondering if you could help me find the book." I was half expecting her to look at me as if I had green scales and twenty-five heads, like some people have. But she didn't. She seemed to know about learning differences. She said, "Sure, come with me." and helped me find it. I wish more people were like her.

When I went to Colorado to a leadership camp with "normal" kids, my experience was not as easy. I was really nervous before I went. We were going to be doing these "team-building" exercises, which I was afraid would reveal my differences.

Some of my worst nightmares did come true there. I cried several times, when I got humiliated because there were things I couldn't understand or do well. There were many times when I wanted to quit, just give up. But what's great is that I got through those moments, I spoke up, and I learned to be really strong. I also climbed a mountain there. You might think, whoop-de-do, but for me it was difficult, and my friend even got hurt on the way down. But that's really what we all do internally—climb mountains, try to get through the struggles one step at time.

During a discussion session at the camp about diversity in our schools, the topic of learning differences came up. This one girl said she felt bad for the special-ed kids in her school, because they got picked on and teased, and they looked up to the so-called normal kids.

I couldn't contain myself. I said, "I have LD. I go to a special school for special education." The room got very quiet. I wanted her to see that I was just like her, except I struggled with academics. She, and the other kids, hadn't known I was different. I think they got to see that LD is not exactly what they thought it was—that kids with LD can be just like them in many ways. We're more like the other kids than they even know: kids got picked on even in my high school, where everyone had LD. Some people even used the word "retard" to hurt other people's feelings. Teenagers can be really mean, with or without LD.

The Struggles That Come with LD

As you can see, kids with LD deal with a lot on top of their difficulty learning—self-consciousness, anxiety. Having to take standardized tests like the SAT even though the odds are stacked against us, having to come up with an answer when someone casually asks how we did on the SAT or where we're going to college. I'm not going to one of the name-brand colleges everyone has heard of. When I tell people where I am going, I try to say it with a lot of confidence. But I realize that most people won't recognize it, and that makes me a little embarrassed, even though I know I should not compare myself to mainstream kids, or to my sister, who takes AP courses and will probably go to one of the top ten colleges in the country.

I feel for my sister, too. It must be hard for her, taking all these intense classes, applying to the name-brand schools, and then feeling restrained about discussing colleges and grades in front of her LD sister. Fortunately, LD doesn't always get in our way. We have close talks about guys and how our day went. We go to the movies, and one time we were having so much fun together there, we *both* almost stepped on the up escalator when we wanted to go down. We get along really well. I love Annie Rose.

Still, there are times when I am very angry at my LD. I want to be able to understand certain things—like algebra—and I want it all to just be easy, and it isn't. That's so frustrating!

The Benefits of LD

But there is another side to it. I've come to accept my LD as just part of who I am. Not only that; I feel like there are good things about it—little things and big things.

For instance, I can read backwards. One day when I was young and having trouble reading, I was in the car with my family when a neon yellow van was behind us. "Ambulance," I said. And my parents looked surprised. The word was written backwards on the front of the ambulance—that way people can read it through their rear-view mirrors. But I was looking at it straight on, and read it backwards. Pretty cool, huh?

But more importantly, LD has made me more sensitive to other people's struggles, and not just other kids with learning differences. It has made me very aware of myself and forced me to pay attention to things in a way I might not have if I had had it easier. It has made me try harder, and, as [British prime minister] Winston Churchill once said, "Never, never, never give up."

Just because you have learning differences doesn't mean you can't prosper. Kids with LD are like flowers. How they are nurtured determines how they'll grow. If their spirits are really supported and motivated, those kids can really bloom.

I know because I was nurtured, supported, and motivated by my mother, my father, and my sister, and I have really bloomed, especially in the last couple of years.

SOCIAL ISSUES
FIRSTHAND

CHAPTER 2

Learning Disabilities
in Family Life

A Mother Discovers Her Daughter's Learning Disability

Anne Ford

When Anne Ford's daughter, Allegra, was finishing her second year of nursery school, the headmistress asked Ms. Ford to attend Parents Day to observe Allegra's behavior. There was some concern among the teachers that Allegra may have learning problems that would be best addressed by a special kindergarten. In the following excerpt from her book about raising her daughter, Ms. Ford eloquently describes the defining moments when a parent begins to realize and accept her child's differences, the permanence of a learning disability, and its impact.

Ms. Ford, great-granddaughter of the founder of Ford Motor Company, has dedicated time and talent on behalf of those with learning differences. Most notably, she has served as chairman emeritus of the Board of the National Center for Learning Disabilities.

I arrived at Parents Day and took my place with the other parents, and there it was in full view, staring me in the face. But did I see it? No. I saw *something*, but not the reality of the situation.

The children were in a small tight circle around the teacher, all faces upturned to hers, all eyes glued to her as they listened to a story she was reading.

One child wasn't there. She was off in a corner on her own, pretending to be cooking lunch for the class, completely oblivious to the story, the teacher, the other children.

She was in her own world. When someone brought her back to the circle she stayed for a moment, but then she was off again, over into the kitchen to play in that other world.

"Now we're going to make the brownies," she said, talking to herself. "You put the mix in the pan and put the pan in the oven." She was teaching class, using the words she had heard another teacher use and imitating the teacher's voice.

I wanted to go to her, to take her back to the group, but I forced myself to watch. Other parents glanced at her from time to time, and then at me . . . and they smiled. What was in those smiles? Sympathy? Or was it the simple joy of watching a little girl playing on her own? I couldn't tell.

During playtime, Allegra was in another area of the room engaged in solitary games with only her imagination as her companion. The other children avoided her—not because they didn't like her, but because they couldn't understand her. She was on her own, but it didn't seem to bother her at all. Her isolation was a result of imaginary games she created in her mind, with rules only she could understand.

I now saw what Miss Zimmerman [the headmistress of Allegra's nursery school] was talking about. I still wasn't alarmed, or even overly concerned, but I was a little embarrassed. Embarrassment is not an easy emotion to feel about your own child and that was the first time I ever felt it. There was nothing wrong with her (as far as I could tell), so why was she acting this way? I was convinced that it was exactly what my mother had already dismissed—a behavior problem. And again, I knew she could overcome it with my help and perhaps a little more discipline.

In Denial

We began on our walk home from school that very afternoon. "Allegra, do you know what the teacher is doing when she gathers you all into a circle?"

"She has a book."

"Yes, and she's reading to you, the same way I do at night. But she wants you to listen. You need to sit with all the other children while she's reading."

I remembered my own problems keeping her still in the bed and wondered if I had contributed to her restlessness by not forcing her to listen to stories that were not about her or *Goodnight Moon*. Was I too lenient? Did I unwittingly encourage this apparent willful distraction?

Even then, on the walk home, that distraction was on display. I spoke to her but her attention wandered. The yellow bus, the blue car, a pigeon, another little girl: all were enough to pull her attention away from my words and my voice. I stopped on the sidewalk and crouched down in front of her. "Allegra," I said, firmly. "You need to listen to me when I'm talking. You need to listen to the teacher when she's talking."

She looked at me intently with her sweet brown eyes and then she glanced over my shoulder at . . . something, I don't know what—and I knew I had lost her again. Still, I had faith in my ability to change her behavior. It was a simple matter of paying attention, that's all. There was nothing wrong with her.

I do not know how much of this early denial was formed by my innate character and how much by attitudes learned when I was growing up, but the combination of the two formed a barrier of defenses around me that was so impenetrable that I did not realize there was any barrier at all. My "reality," the reality I was trying to will into existence, was that Allegra had no problems at all and that there was nothing to upset the perfect world I imagined for my children and myself.

This denial would grow stronger in the coming months, but in some ways it served a useful purpose. Denial is not a completely negative reaction, at least not in the beginning and in small doses. Theoretically it may be preferable to be clear-eyed and realistic right from the start but this rarely happens. Unless you have a child with a disability it is difficult to imagine the crushing pain and sense of panic that can come with this awful realization. So many things come upon you at the same time. "It can't be," you tell yourself over and over again, "it *can't* be!" The implications are so vast that it is difficult to take them in all at once. Denial may be nature's way of easing us into a process of acceptance.

Sometimes a parent's denial can be so strong it impacts the child in negative ways. The parent may seriously delay getting help for the child, for example, or refuse to seek help at all. This parent may repeatedly force the child into situations where he or she fails, all in a long, futile effort to prove there is nothing wrong. I never went quite that far with Allegra (though I came close). For me, denial was manifested in an inability to accept reality even as I made an honest attempt to deal with it. It was sort of like, "All right, I'll face the problem and deal with it, even though I know there is no problem at all."

Hanging on to the Denial

My war between denial and acceptance began on Parents Day. It was waged within me from that moment onward, with each getting the upper hand at various times in the coming months.

Not long after Parents Day, I happened to pass Allegra's bedroom and saw that her door was closed. That was rather unusual and I wondered if she was all right. I reached for the door handle but stopped at the sound of her voice. "Goodnight moon," I heard. "Goodnight stars. . ."

I opened her door. She was sitting on a stool in the middle of the bedroom. Her dolls and teddy bears were arranged in a semi-circle in front of her. "Hi Sweetheart," I said as I entered the room. "What are you doing?"

"Playing school," she returned, and I realized that she was the teacher and the dolls were the students.

"Are you reading to them?" I asked.

"Yes. I'm reading *Goodnight Moon*." She held the book in her hand, but it was upside down. I smiled at her; she had obviously memorized the story, and I thought it was so cute that she was holding the book upside down.

"Are they listening to you?" I asked.

"Oh, yes, Mommy. They're being very good."

"That's wonderful, Allegra," I said, and I smiled again as I left her to her students. I closed the door, but not all the way. I stood in the hall and listened as my daughter, the child who could not sit still, became the teacher and read to the class. And then I heard this: "Come back now. You need to pay attention."

As she had when cooking lunch for the class during Parents Day, she repeated the words she knew best, focusing on one doll in the circle. "Come back now," she said. "Pay attention. You have to sit down and listen while I read the story. Why are you wandering off again. . . ?"

I now knew that she was aware of what was happening in her school. She knew the rules, how to sit down, how to pay attention. She knew enough to ask it of her dolls. So why couldn't she do it herself?

Day after day I heard her talking to her dolls and one day I asked if I could join her. I sat on the floor as if I was one of her students. When she pretended that one of the dolls walked away from the reading circle I asked if she had ever done that.

"Sometimes," she told me.

"Do you know why?"

She didn't answer.

"Allegra? Do you know why you walk away from the reading circle?"

"Do you think my doll's dress is pretty?"

"Yes, Allegra, it's beautiful. Why do you walk away from the circle, sweetheart?"

"I think her red dress is pretty, too."

The Evaluation

Miss Zimmerman called me with the name of a diagnostician. "It's only an evaluation," she said. "Nothing to be worried about."

I wasn't worried. Allegra would pass. I knew she would.

The evaluation was simple enough. They asked me questions about her background and family life: "Does she have brothers and sisters? Older or younger? Is there any indication that her brother or any other family member has had difficulty in school?" They reviewed a report submitted by the nursery school. They administered intelligence and ability tests, asking her to identify basic shapes and colors, simple number sequences and rhymes. They asked her to say the alphabet and put together simple puzzles. There were gross motor skill tests such as running around obstacles and balancing on one foot for five to ten seconds. Fine motor skill tests included building a tower of small blocks and copying circles. This was followed with communication skill tests such as understanding sentences involving time concepts like "tomorrow" or size comparisons like "big or bigger." They asked her if she understood what it meant when she was told, "Let's pretend. . . ."

Allegra did fine on colors and some shapes, the same with rhyming. She had difficulty with number sequences and with both the gross and fine motor skills, and she was completely unable to understand time and size concepts, or even understand "let's pretend." She didn't know what "let's pretend" meant. For Allegra, everything was based in the reality of the moment, and that included imaginary situations. If another child said, "Let's pretend a bear is behind that tree," there was no "pretend" at all for her. She was convinced a real bear was there and about to chase her. I always considered that to be a positive trait, the result of a very active and healthy imagination.

Then they asked me about her medical history. "Were there any problems at birth?"

"No," I said. "Not for her anyway."

"Were there problems for you?"

"No. Well, maybe a little problem, but nothing important. I had an epidural, but for some reason it didn't work. My doctor injected me again and again, but it still didn't work." I hesitated. "You don't think that caused any trouble do you?"

"No, I doubt it," the diagnostician said. "Anything else?"

"Not that I remember," I said. "She was smaller than her brother. Her birth weight was a pound less than his. Oh, and she had pneumonia when she was about a month old."

"I see. Was she deprived of oxygen?"

"No," I said in surprise. "No, they put her in a tent. I'm sure she wasn't deprived of oxygen."

"Did they give her the heel test?"

"What's that?"

"It is standard procedure to prick a child's heel to check for slow or nonexistent reflexes, a sign of oxygen deprivation."

I told them I didn't know if the test had been administered, but that I would look into it. I had never heard of it before. I later learned that no one gave her the test. No one asked if I wanted it done. I never asked for it because I never heard of it. There was no way to know if she was deprived of oxygen.

The evaluation was concluded and the official results came back. She was found to have a "variable level of functioning, being below her age expectation."

A horrible-sounding phrase. "What does that mean?" I asked the doctor.

"It may not mean a lot now, but I do agree with Miss Zimmerman. I believe she needs some special help before going on to first grade. A special kindergarten."

"Special . . . what does that mean?" I asked. "There's nothing really wrong with her, is there?"

"No, not yet, but—"

"So there's nothing to worry about, right? She's going to be fine. There's nothing wrong." My questions were not questions at all: they were statements designed to cover the diagnosis with solid reassurance. I refused to believe what I was told. I was her mother. If there was a serious problem, surely I would recognize it. I knew I would. I had already convinced myself that she had only a small behavior problem, a minor matter of distraction, an overactive imagination. I heard her with her dolls. I knew she could sit down and stay still. I knew it was possible for her to pay attention. I could help her. I could work with her, and show her how to put the puzzles together over and over again. The pieces would fall into place. Everything would fall into place. I knew it would.

Denial Shattered in an Instant

This belief changed and my first defensive wall of denial was forcibly shattered on a late December afternoon when all the parents and siblings of the forty or so children in the nursery school gathered together in the auditorium at the Madison Avenue Presbyterian Church.

It was the annual Christmas Pageant.

There aren't too many things more funny or heartwarming than the sound of small children belting out loud off-key renditions of "Jingle Bells" or "Here Comes Santa Claus." I knew that my sister and mother would have enjoyed the pageant, but I did not ask them to come. I was still upset and a little hurt by the doctor's suggestions—I didn't believe Allegra had a serious problem but her inattentive behavior (which I couldn't ignore) was enough to instill some doubt. Could she stand in a structured line and sing a song? Yes, I knew she could, but *would* she? She could perform, but would she follow all the directions? I did not know the answers, and so I decided to go to the performance alone.

I can still picture the auditorium, but I have no memory of what songs were sung or what Allegra was wearing. I was sitting in the darkness in the middle of the audience. The curtains opened and the lights came up on the stage.

I couldn't see her at first. It took a moment to sort out the children.

They began to sing the first song and that's when it happened. In one instant, all the illusions I had about my daughter, the fears, even my own ignorance about her true nature, careened together in one single, heart-stopping moment.

The children were grouped together with the music director conducting, her back to the audience. All of a sudden, out of nowhere, Allegra appeared at the front of the stage and began to dance and sing a song. I couldn't hear what she was singing, but I knew it had nothing to do with what the others were singing. For me the entire world collapsed into a single moment frozen in time—my daughter standing out in front, lost and bewildered, singing something known only to her. And there I am, watching her from deep within the dark auditorium, separated from her by chairs and people, unable to reach her and hold her and take away those feelings of confusion. It was a moment frozen in time, but the feelings and impact of this moment were almost entirely internal. They were my feelings, and my perceptions. No one pointed at Allegra and laughed. Stunned silence did not fall in the auditorium. Very little happened at all. The music teacher simply reached for her arm and gently pulled her back to the group. A few of the parents did chuckle a bit, thinking it was cute and funny to see a child so expressive and extroverted she couldn't help but take center stage. I might have joined them had I not heard the recent reports from the doctor and headmistress. I, too, might have found it cute and funny. But I didn't. I saw for the first time how right they were. And I knew that what was cute and funny today would not be cute and funny tomorrow.

She had no clue she was doing something out of the ordinary. She did not know how inappropriate her behavior was. She had no idea that she had just shown me, for the first time, that the dreams I had of my daughter as a perfect little school girl were unlikely to come true.

Siblings with Different Needs

Dana Buchman

In her autobiography, A Special Education: One Family's Journey through the Maze of Learning Disabilities, *Dana Buchman shares the challenges she and her husband, Tom, faced raising a learning disabled child. Buchman admits to the demands of her career as a clothing designer. Always ambitious, she found the demands of parenting, especially complicated because of her daughter's learning difficulties, often conflicted with the pressures of her job. Very honestly, Buchman details her sometimes unsuccessful attempts to juggle both. In the following excerpt from her book, she relates the typical strain that often exists between siblings when one is learning disabled and the dilemmas facing concerned parents.*

Tom and I were talking recently, and he brought up how hard it must be for each of the girls—how difficult it must be for Charlotte to have her younger sister reach many milestones before she does, and how awkward it must be for Annie, as the younger sister, to lead. Annie often feels like the older sister, and Charlotte, like the younger. It's funny—I remember now that when they used to play house, Charlotte always got to be the mother or the big sister. They seemed to be agreeing to let Charlotte play the role she was supposed to, as determined by birth order.

Life isn't fair, especially when you put LD [learning disabilities] into the mix. It isn't fair to have LD when your sibling doesn't, and that leads to anger and jealousy, on top of the frustration and anguish that come with LD in the first place. It's also not fair to be a sibling of an LD child. You have to watch your parents devote an inordinate amount of time and attention to the "different" child, and that incites anger and jealousy, not to mention guilt for being the "normal" one.

A few years ago, Annie got very angry that Charlotte consistently came home from school with much less homework than she. Just getting through the school day is a huge challenge for Charlotte. There's so much for her to negotiate: finding her way to and from her special school, managing conversations with different people, absorbing the lessons of the day. By the time she gets home, she's listless and she needs a nap. Annie, on the other hand, goes to one of the most competitive private schools in New York City; she's involved in after-school sports and other extracurricular activities. And when she gets home, she faces hours upon hours of challenging homework in all of her subjects.

One day, Annie said to Charlotte, "It's not fair! How come you don't have to do as much work as I do? I come home and do homework for hours and hours, and you only have a very little bit to do."

Charlotte was completely taken aback. She paused a minute and then said, "Oh, really? You think I have it easy? You want to be me?"

Who won that battle? Neither of them.

Resentments

Lately, the deep-seated resentments on both their parts are coming to the surface more often. This is actually good news! Better to air things, we are all learning.

For example, one evening the year before Charlotte went off to college, we were all gathered at home for dinner. Annie came to the table from doing her calculus homework and was explaining something she found interesting about the delta function. I vaguely followed the gist of what she was saying, calling up remnants of what I had learned in calculus through the fog of thirty-five years, but I was not able to engage in the details of it. I enjoyed that she was excited about it, but when everyone came to the dinner table, the talk turned to other things.

More specifically, our talk turned to Charlotte's acceptance to Curry College, one of the few colleges that has a really comprehensive LD program. Tom and I were congratulating her and sharing her enjoyment at having been accepted, especially because Charlotte had been agonizing over whether she'd get into any schools with her very low SAT scores. And she had been feeling awkward about telling people the unfamiliar names of the colleges that had LD programs, which she was waiting to hear from. Annie, meanwhile, was already looking at "name" schools like Brown, Harvard, and Dartmouth, which depressed Charlotte.

As dinner ended that evening, and Annie left the table to start her homework, I could sense something was wrong, so I followed her into her room. I don't remember how she started, but it became clear very quickly that she was angry. She said, "You all get so excited at every little thing that Charlotte does, like writing her paper. But then when I get an A- in Calculus, which I think is pretty good, you say, 'Oh, that's nice.' And you say things like 'Well, I took Calculus and forgot it the day the class ended, and it's not something I've ever used anyway.' So it makes it seem like this thing I'm interested in has no value. I don't get the credit for the things I do well, and yet Charlotte gets credit for things she does well. In fact, she gets credit for just even trying to do things. I get a high score on the PSAT and you say, 'That's nice.'"

Realization

My spine went cold. I knew exactly what she was talking about. Annie was right. I have often minimized the importance of her achievements. My twisted reasoning went this way: if Annie worked hard and made A's in very difficult subjects, and I got overly excited, I would belie the story I was telling Charlotte and myself that grades and academic achievement don't matter.

I have always told the girls that grades don't matter, that if they do their homework and do their best, then that's enough. I always asked if they knew what grades I made in high school biology. Or what I got on my SAT's. Of course not, they'd say. And neither did anyone else in the world, certainly not the women who buy my clothes. What do they care about how well I did in calculus? Although I did well in school, grades ultimately never affected my career or my life with Tom or with my friends.

But I carried way too far my commitment to telling the girls that their achievement in school did not matter to me, that trying to do the work and enjoying the learning were what was important. In putting across that message to Annie, I failed to delight in her academic and athletic gifts in the way I delighted in Charlotte's unconventional, nonacademic gifts. I didn't make it clear that I loved that she skis like the wind, gracefully and confidently. That she learns easily and enjoys her prowess. And that she has always been kind and patient with her sister. But, for every frustration of Annie's, Charlotte had two. Some of the most basic things were huge challenges for her—things like keeping up with the conversation at dinner.

For a long time, we didn't realize Charlotte was having a hard time keeping up with us in conversation and that we needed to create openings for her. At the dinner table, Tom and Annie and I would just start rattling off what our days were like, talking quickly, using big words, and Charlotte would sit there, dumbfounded, not knowing how to organize her thoughts and get a word in edgewise. We finally realized that we needed to make the space for her to speak. But then we ran into another problem: Charlotte would take up the whole dinner hour telling a story. And now there was no way for anyone else to talk. How could we kindly and gently rein her in, after working so hard to make it easier for her to speak up, so that the rest of us got a chance to contribute to the dinner conversation? It was tricky.

Charlotte also has to live with constantly measuring herself against her little sister. I remember the night that Annie came back from taking the written test for her driver's permit. Charlotte had taken it a few months before and just passed. At dinner that night, Charlotte asked Annie, "So, how many questions did you get wrong?" It was a loaded question, and we were all silent for a moment before Annie quietly answered. Of course, Annie got a perfect score on the exam. Of course, Charlotte, who had barely passed the test herself, suspected that. Charlotte was venting her anger by provoking Annie's guilt.

Managing Emotions

So, how do you handle all this emotional mess? For one thing, I got help. I'm a fan of professional help: call in a designer when you need help getting dressed, and call in a shrink when you need help figuring out a psychological issue!

At one point, when Annie was six, it became impossible to dismiss the fact that she and I weren't getting along. I took her to see Charlotte's neuropsychologist, even though Annie wasn't the one with neurological issues.

It was like we were in couples counseling, my daughter and I. We were angry at each other, and we didn't know why. The neuropsychologist, Michele, had Annie draw a picture. Annie drew a tree whose leaves had all turned brown and fallen to the ground. (It makes me teary even to write that.) To a psychological professional, that is a loud and clear message of sadness in a little person. From that, I learned that Charlotte's needs were overshadowing Annie's, especially for attention and acknowledgment. This was the beginning of my awareness of the imbalance in our family loft.

Probably the best remedy for that imbalance has been making time for Charlotte and Annie separately. I started to realize that it was often easier, and a richer experience for me, to be with one child at a time. I would take each of them out individually on a weekend afternoon. I would take extra time putting them each to bed at night, something that was difficult because I got so little sleep myself. I was often up from 2 to 4 a.m. sketching because it was the only time when it was peaceful enough for me to relax and free-associate creatively. I also often had to get up at crazy hours to speak with our offices in Asia.

Indeed, my work was everpresent, but in one respect, I managed to combine it with the needs of each of my daughters: I'd let each of the girls take turns traveling with me to trunk shows around the country. In that environment, I could pamper each of them, one at a time. The trip would usually include a limousine ride, room service, a bubble bath, and then the excitement of joining me for my appearance at a store. For Charlotte, this was especially fun. Away from home at a trunk show, where all my customers would fuss over her, she could be just a normal girl. No one had to know she couldn't do math easily or read maps, or that she had differences of any kind.

Divvying Things Up

Something very interesting has happened between the girls as they have grown up: they each sort of naturally chose the areas in which they were strongest, and neither would ever trespass on the other's field.

For example, when Charlotte was six and Annie was four, we started taking the girls skiing. I'll be very honest here: I don't like to ski. I wasn't always so honest, though. Poor Tom, I gave him the impression that I loved it, from the beginning of our relationship. I learned to ski in college, more or less as a way to meet guys. I thought it was something you were supposed to like, so I made myself seem enthusiastic about it.

I similarly thought it would be a good thing for Charlotte and Annie to learn. Skiing is a very social sport. And Tom really loves it.

At first, both girls seemed to take to it. They enjoyed their beginner lessons. But as Annie began to advance, Charlotte started to show some resistance.

It didn't help that one very insensitive ski instructor humiliated her by comparing her to Annie and other kids, out loud. They were taking a group lesson, and toward the end, the instructor discussed their levels. He said, of Annie and her friend, "Okay, these two are the best." Of Charlotte he said, somewhat callously, "She's last."

That was the end of skiing for Charlotte. Tom offered several times to help her, one-on-one. She took him up on it once or twice, but then declared herself a nonskier.

I asked her recently whether she remembered what motivated that choice. Was it just that she didn't like skiing? Or was it the distinction between herself and her sister?

"Annie was better," Charlotte stated very simply. "I didn't want to do it because she was much better."

So, Annie got skiing. That's her thing. And she's awfully good at it. Charlotte and I have become expert at *après ski*. As I've mentioned before, we spend the whole time in the lodge, either reading or doing arts projects together.

Annie won't touch art. That's Charlotte's. Annie used to enjoy being creative with Charlotte and me, but somewhere along the line, she gave it up. I recently asked her about that, too. She said, "I let Charlotte have art. I like art, but it's not like I'm repressing some great talent or burning desire. I'd rather let that be Charlotte's area."

It was a mixed blessing, this division of labor—positive in that they don't want to be competitive with one another, and each wants to let the other shine; negative in that they are both confined to one area or another without feeling free to try everything. But, I suppose, it's all part of how we get along.

CHAPTER 3

Learning Disabilities in the Clinic

Identifying Each Patient's Disability Is Essential

Mel Levine, M.D.

Mel Levine is a Harvard-educated, developmental-behavioral pediatrician who, by his own admission, finds it very difficult to cut paper with scissors and has never been able to fold an 8½ by 11 inch piece of paper so that it will fit into an envelope. Exceedingly bright, but dealing with undiagnosed learning disabilities, he had his share of what he calls "the horror and the pain of humiliation" during his school years.

When Levine directed the outpatient clinic at Children's Hospital in Boston, he found that many young patients did not have illness or disease but, instead, problems with school and life skills. He observed that: "They appeared to me to be neither emotionally disturbed, nor dumb, nor lazy; there was obviously something far more subtle and insidious going on inside them, something awaiting our detection and good management." He went on to base his career on helping these children. In 1995 he became cofounder (with Charles Schwab) of All Kinds of Minds, a nonprofit institute that trains teachers and informs parents, clinicians, and children about learning differences.

Levine maintains that, quite aside from the more commonly known learning disabilities, such as dyslexia and dyscalculia, there are a variety of neurological systems that affect our thinking and ability—or inability—to learn. In the following excerpt, he describes a patient whose problems with sequential ordering made time management a constant strain.

Parents may be perplexed by the realization that their child's life is somehow "out of order"—from getting herself dressed to reciting the alphabet. She meets havoc throughout the school day, bewildered by teachers' rapid volleys of multi-step directions and expectations for efficient sequential output. She may find it hard to organize her thoughts to present them orally in coherent steps. She most likely feels defective and markedly inferior to peers. Here's a typical brief biography of such a needlessly suffering ego:

Joann's parents arrived at the indisputable conclusion that this gusher of pure charm didn't know the meaning of the word "time." When I first saw Joann in my office, she was eleven, a very anxious and withdrawn student from northern New Jersey. She was always out of time and never known to be on time or even close to functioning in step with time. To Joann, schedules of any sort were cloudy notions, and deadlines were vague and forgettable goals at best. She was in a perpetual time warp, inevitably unaware of when she was running behind or getting ahead (the latter a most rare occurrence). Interestingly and not at all unusual, her father had a similar lack of orientation in time. Joann's mother said the two of them made her tear out her hair when the family needed to go someplace; Dad and daughter were never in a state of readiness. In fact, I'm pretty sure the problem caused Joann's father, a furniture designer, to lose two jobs and to be passed over for promotion once. He confessed that he did everything at the last minute and often missed important deadlines. He had a reputation for being unreliable at work, even though the drawings he ultimately produced were quite good. Too bad this man never knew he had a lifelong sequencing problem—that is, until we discussed Joann's glitches. He could have worked on them and saved himself a lot of agony. That happens all too often in my office. I discuss a child's dysfunctions, and one or both parents recognize themselves in what I'm saying.

Reliably late for all dates and appointments, to this day Joann remains unsure about the order of the months of the year and often gets mixed up when given three or four things in a row to do in school or at home. As a preschooler and well into early elementary school, Joann had trouble reckoning with the order of days of the week and sequences of steps in various math procedures. This child was noticeably late learning to tell time and is still hesitant in doing so (her digital watch has been a lifesaver). Throughout elementary school, Joann was told over and over again that she wasn't really trying. She was made to feel that her tardiness and disorganization were her fault, that she had a bad attitude. On frequent occasions she told her mother that she didn't much like herself.

School Evaluations Didn't Uncover the Problem

In kindergarten and first grade, Joann became disoriented when sentences contained temporal prepositions, such as "before" and "after." For instance, she once told her dad, "I hope you get home late tonight so we can play together outside before it gets dark." Joann has always excelled in science. She currently loves her physics class and has gotten As in all her science courses. She wants to be either a geophysicist or an anthropologist. She is universally popular. A deft athlete, she also has a passionate interest and high skill level in Scottish Highlands dancing. But in school Joann struggles with anything requiring sequencing, a fact no one has observed. In third grade and fifth grade she was evaluated for possible learning disabilities but, because there was no significant difference between her IQ and her achievement test scores, she was deemed ineligible for any services and determined not to be learning disabled. But no one ever said what she was!

The way we test for learning disabilities is especially irrational, since there has never been much agreement regarding what learning disability is. This kind of nonsense goes on all the time, as all sorts of invalid formulas are used to determine who has a genuine right to be helped and who does not.

Joann was victimized by her school's special formula. Her parents were totally confused. After all, if she's not LD [learning disabled], then she must be stupid or hopelessly lazy. What else is there?

I met Joann shortly after her second school evaluation, after which her mother declared, "Nobody understands this girl. I know there's something going on here, and it's being dreadfully overlooked." Our team tested Joann. From her history I suspected she might be struggling with sequencing. This was soon confirmed. When I showed Joann a series of different shapes and pointed to each of these in a particular order, she was unable to remember and re-create the order. She could only retain a sequence of three objects but she should have been able to remember five or six. She also had trouble repeating numbers in the correct order. By the time we were nearly finished with our various sequential ordering tasks, I could see tears welling up in Joann's eyes. It's amazing how often a child's sad moods and feelings come forth and become amplified when confronting a specific area of weakness. So, out of compassion, I promptly quit this pursuit and switched to something she could do well. Joann bounced back.

A Plan of Action Brings Results

Once we pinpointed Joann's troubles with sequential ordering, we were able to make recommendations. The first was to help her understand the nature of her sequencing trouble. Ann Hobgood, our educational diagnostician met with Joann several times and talked to her over the telephone regularly. Joann was encouraged to be especially alert in the presence of sequences, to visualize while people were talking to her in sequences, and to whisper under her breath. She also was taught to make flow diagrams to help her think about different sequential processes in math and science. Because of her past lack of progress, Joann was taken out of school, and her mother home-schooled her for two years, during which time she made dramatic gains in her overall academic performance, her sequencing strategies, and her organizational practices. Back in a regular school program in eighth grade, she continued to thrive academically.

Now nearly seventeen, Joann has learned to apply computer graphics effectively; she creates flow charts, timelines, and other such diagrammatic representations to help her learn and remember processes or events that take place in a specific serial order. Her parents, after coming to understand the nature of their daughter's neurodevelopmental dysfunction, encouraged her to exploit her keen spatial abilities to compensate for her unreliable sequencing. Joann made that discovery herself. After years of struggling at the bottom of her class, Joann's stock is starting to rise. Much of this acceleration resulted when one perceptive teacher finally sat down and reviewed with Joann the fact that she had all the abilities she needed to succeed in life but that she was being hampered by problems with sequential ordering. Joann felt redeemed; her motivation was restored and she was able to make much better use of her admirable assets.

Why Some Smart People Can't Read

Sally Shaywitz, M.D.

Sally Shaywitz is one of the foremost experts on dyslexia. She is a neuroscientist who has brought her expertise to several positions including professor of pediatrics at Yale, codirector of the Yale Center for the Study of Learning and Attention, and a member of the National Reading Panel, organized to ascertain the most effective reading programs.

In the following excerpt, Shaywitz offers details about two of her patients, explaining why she believes some people of normal or above normal intelligence have great difficulty deciphering the written word. She offers her theory that phonological processing—the ability to distinguish the distinctive sounds of language—is essential for reading. She considers dyslexia a "localized weakness within a specific component" rather than a generalized difficulty with language.

I want you to meet two of my patients, Alex and Gregory. Alex is ten years old, and Gregory, a medical student, just celebrated his twenty-third birthday. Their experiences are typical of children and young adults with dyslexia. You will learn how Alex's and Gregory's seemingly diverse symptoms— trouble reading, absolute terror of reading aloud, problems spelling, difficulties finding the right word, mispronouncing words, rote memory nightmares—represent the expression of a single, isolated weakness. At the same time you will learn that other intellectual abilities—thinking, reasoning, understanding—are untouched by dyslexia. This contrasting pattern produces the paradox of dyslexia: profound and persistent difficulties experienced by some very bright people in learning to read. I am emphasizing the strengths of the dyslexic because there is often a tendency to underestimate his abilities. The reading problem is often glaringly apparent while the strengths may be more subtle and overlooked. . . .

Alex's Story

In his first years of life, Alex was so quick to catch on to things that his parents were surprised when he struggled to learn his letters in kindergarten. When shown a letter, he would stare, frown, and then randomly guess. He couldn't seem to learn the letter names. In first grade he struggled to link letters with their sounds. By the third grade Alex continued to stammer and sputter as he tried to decipher what was on the page in front of him. Language had clearly become a struggle for Alex. He seemed to understand a great deal, yet he was not always articulate. He mispronounced many words, leaving off the beginning (*lephant* for elephant) or the ends of words, or inverting the order within a word (*emeny* for enemy). Alex had trouble finding the exact word he wanted to say even though it seemed he could tell you all about it. One evening he was trying to explain about sharks living in the ocean:

> The water, the water, lots of water, salty water with big fish, it's a lotion. No, no, that's not what I mean. Oh, you know, it's on all the maps, it's a lotion—ocean, that's what it is—a sea, no big sea, it's an ocean, an ocean!

Looking at this handsome, very serious little boy who could spend hours putting together complex puzzles and assembling intricate model airplanes, his father could not believe that Alex had a problem. Alex, however, became increasingly aware of his difficulty reading and asked more and more frequently why all his friends were in a different reading group. He practiced, he tried, but it just never seemed to come out right.

His parents brought him to the Yale Center [the Yale Center for the Study of Learning and Attention at the Yale School of Medicine, New Haven, Connecticut] for evaluation. We learned that Alex was extremely smart, scoring in the gifted range in abstract reasoning and in logic. His vocabulary was also highly developed. Alex could learn, he could reason, and he could understand concepts at a very high level. Despite these strengths, his performance in reading words was dismal; for example, he was able to read only ten out of twenty-four words on a third grade level. What gave Alex the most difficulty, however, was nonsense words (made-up words that can be pronounced; for example, *gern, ruck*). He struggled to decipher these words. Sometimes he used the first letter to generate a response (such as *glim* for *gern*, *rold* for *ruck*); at other times it seemed as if he just gave up, making seemingly random guesses. In contrast, Alex was able to read a short passage silently and answer questions about it far better than he was able to read and pronounce isolated single words. In reading a passage silently to himself, Alex made good use of clues such as pictures in the book and the surrounding words; he used them to get to the meaning of sentences and passages that contained words he could not read. "I picture what it says," he explained. However, Alex sparkled when asked to *listen* to a story and then respond to a series of questions, scoring significantly above average. Reading aloud was particularly painful for Alex. He was reluctant to read in front of the class, and it was easy to understand why. His reading was labored; words were mispronounced, substituted, or often omitted entirely. Words that he correctly read in one sentence would be misread in a subsequent sentence. He read excruciatingly slowly and haltingly. Increasingly, Alex would ask to go to the bathroom when it was nearing his turn to read. If called upon, he often acted silly making the words into a joke or tumbling himself onto the floor and laughing so that he would be sent out of the room.

Poor spelling skills were compounded by his almost illegible handwriting. Letters were large, misshapen, and wobbly. In contrast, Alex's math skills, particularly problem solving and reasoning abilities, were in the superior range. At the close of the testing, Alex diagnosed his own reading problem: "I don't know the sounds the letters make." Furthermore, he told the evaluator that it bothered him that his friends were in a different reading group. Sometimes, he said, this made him very sad. His one wish was to be a better reader, but he didn't know exactly how that would happen.

When I met with Alex's parents, they had many questions: Does he have a problem? If so, what is the nature of the problem? What could be done to help him? Above all, they asked, "Will he be all right?" I reassured them that Alex would not only survive, he would thrive.

Gregory's Story

In the course of my work, I have evaluated for reading disabilities not only hundreds of children but also scores of young adult men and women. Their histories provide a picture of what the future will be for a bright child like Alex who happens to be dyslexic. Gregory was a grown-up Alex. Gregory came to see me after experiencing a series of difficulties in his first-year medical courses. He was quite discouraged.

Although he had been diagnosed as dyslexic in grade school, Gregory had also been placed in a program for gifted students. His native intelligence, together with extensive support and tutoring, had enabled him to graduate from high school with honors and gain admission to an Ivy League college. In college Gregory had worked hard to compensate for his disability and eventually received offers from several top medical schools. Now, however, he was beginning to doubt his own ability. He had no trouble comprehending the intricate relationships among physiological systems or the complex mechanisms of disease; indeed, he excelled in those areas that required reasoning skills. More difficult for him was pronouncing long words or novel terms (such as labels used in anatomic descriptions); perhaps his least-well-developed skill was that of rote memorization.

Both Gregory and his professors were perplexed by the inconsistencies in his performance. How could someone who understood difficult concepts so well have trouble with the smaller and simpler details? I explained that Gregory's dyslexia (he was still a slow reader) could account for his inability to name tissue types and body parts in the face of his excellent reasoning skills. His history fit the clinical picture of dyslexia as it has been traditionally defined: an unexpected difficulty learning to read despite intelligence, motivation, and education. Furthermore, I was able to reassure him that because scientists now understand the basic nature of dyslexia, they have been able to devise highly effective strategies to help those with the disorder. I told Gregory that dyslexia reflects a problem within the language system in the brain. The understanding of the central role of language in reading and, particularly, in dyslexia is relatively recent.

Why Alex and Gregory Have Trouble Reading

Explanations of dyslexia that were put forth beginning in the 1920s and that have continued until recently held that defects in the visual system were to blame for the reversals of letters and words thought to typify dyslexia. Eye training was often prescribed to overcome these alleged visual defects. Subsequent research has shown, however, that in contrast to a popular myth, children with dyslexia are not unusually prone to *seeing* letters or words backward and that the deficit responsible for the disorder resides in the language system. These poor readers, like Alex, do have significant difficulty, however, in *naming* the letters, often referring to a *b* as a *d* or reading *saw* as *was*. The problem is a linguistic one, not a visual one.

As noted earlier, dyslexia represents a specific difficulty, with reading, not with thinking skills. Comprehending spoken language is often at a very high level, as it was for Alex, as are other higher-level reasoning skills. Dyslexia is a localized problem.

Understanding that dyslexia reflected a language problem and not a general weakness in intelligence or a primary visual impairment represented a major step forward. Further advances have clarified the nature of the language impairment. Dyslexia does not reflect an overall defect in language but, rather, a localized weakness within a specific component of the language system: the phonologic module. The word *phonologic* is derived from the Greek word *phone,* meaning *sound* (as in *phonograph* and *telephone*). The phonologic module is the language factory, the functional part of the brain where the sounds of language are put together to form words and where words are broken down into their elemental sounds.

Over the past two decades a model of dyslexia has emerged that is based on phonological processing—processing the distinctive sounds of language. The phonologic model is consistent both with how dyslexia manifests itself and with what neuroscientists know about brain organization and function. Researchers at the Yale Center and elsewhere have had an opportunity to test and refine this model through reading and, more recently, brain imaging studies. We and other dyslexia researchers have found that the phonologic model provides a cogent explanation as to why some very smart people have trouble learning to read.

CHAPTER 4

Learning Disabilities in the Classroom

Learning from Experiences in the Classroom

Joan Shapiro and Rebecca Rich

Joan Shapiro and Rebecca Rich both hold doctorate degrees in special education and have done extensive work in programs for learning disabled students. In their book, Facing Learning Disabilities in the Adult Years, *they write about many of the learning disabled individuals they met and treated through the years. Shapiro and Rich write: "Each person has found his or her own way to cope with the disability by 'reframing' the problem into positive solutions. The disability has nevertheless played a significant role in each of their lives." In the following excerpt, they offer a portrait of Michael, a special education teacher, who describes his inability to read fluently. He talks about his own work as an instructor and his belief that "love is the most important technique."*

Michael is a twenty-five-year-old special education teacher who has just completed a master's degree in elementary and special education. He maintained a solid A average in graduate school. This fall [1999], Michael will be again teaching at a special school for children with learning disabilities.

Michael's father, brother, and sister all have a history of learning disabilities. Michael was first diagnosed at the age of eight, when he was in third grade. He was referred to the school-based committee on special education because of difficulty mastering reading and writing skills. Michael remembers that his silent reading was slow and his oral reading hesitant and labored, with little attention to punctuation and phrasing. He had great difficulty mastering phonic skills, which affected his ability, both to decode and to spell. When first told he had a learning disability, Michael reportedly felt confused: "No one really explained what a learning disability was."

Michael received resource-room support services until he graduated from high school. He remembers his greatest difficulty being with reading:

> I would read a whole page of text and have little understanding. Reading aloud . . . well, I hated reading aloud because it reflected my trouble with decoding. My writing was variable, as my content was always good but I had trouble with mechanics. I was generally fine with mathematics, although fractions were hard. I never did master fractions. All in all, my first five years in school were torture. During the summer, on the other hand, I was free from the songs that haunted me: "Moron, dummy, what's wrong with you, everyone else can do it, stop acting so stupid."

Michael describes his school experience, overall, as follows:

> It was a source of a lot of anger. I was a truly horrible student until sixth grade, when my father died. Something changed for me following my father's death. I wanted to help my family. The only thing I could think of was to take care of my own learning. I wanted to be known as smart. I began to work so hard. And I had help. I had wonderful resource-room teachers who taught me strategies. But most importantly they were very supportive. They made me feel good about myself. I could yell and curse at them, and let out all my frustrations, and they would understand. It was not that I didn't respect them. In fact, I respected them more than anyone. They made me feel safe.
>
> Unfortunately, in the classroom I wasn't always safe. In fact, I remember one incident in junior high school that still sends shivers up my spine. It was the first day of school. I was sitting in my seat in English class suddenly nauseated as each student was called upon to read aloud. My life as I saw

it was soon to come to an end. I can't do this. Sweat began to seep through my pores and sizzle upon the surface of my forehead.

I watched as the teacher scanned the room to select a row of readers. As his head spun in my direction, I dropped my pencil on the floor. I have affectionately come to call this the "submarine," one of the evasive tactics in my repertoire. The teacher called my name. I wasn't safe. While I fumbled through the pages, it became apparent to the entire class that I had no idea where we were. "Page 13," the teacher called out, as I continued to search. "We'll come back to you," he said. I was off the hook, but only for the time being. He began again with the front of the row and I knew there would be no getting around this twice. I would have to read.

I could hear the girl three seats ahead of me reading aloud. She read beautifully and, for a second, I forgot the horror of my situation. The words from her mouth flowed softly and gently. She caught every nuance and expressed each emotion. "There's no way that this is the first time she's read this," I thought.

Just then it occurred to me that I could read over the parts that I would be asked to read. I figured that with the two people left between me and the girl who was reading now, I should have just enough time to preread the two pages that would be assigned to me. I skipped ahead and began to practice.

As the person directly in front of me was called upon, I could feel my heart pound at my chest and neck. Continuing to read over what I thought would be my part, I gained in hope and confidence. It was now my turn. I gripped my book tight. "Michael," he bellowed, "skip ahead to page 28. . . ." I lost all feeling in my hands, and the pages slipped through my fingers. This can't be happening. There was nothing left to do but read. I picked the book up, turned to page 28, and began to read.

At first I did all right and, despite a few chuckles at my monotone interpretation, I felt quite proud of myself. As I read on, I decided that I was going to read like my predecessor, who had read with grace and fluidity. However, the harder I tried to read like my peers, the more I sounded as though I belonged back in my first-grade reading group, the Bluejays.

The class laughed and laughed, louder and louder. The teacher yelled. The bell rang. The book fell from my hands. I said nothing. I never returned to that classroom. That night, I cried myself to sleep.

My greatest growth was in high school. The time from sophomore year to senior was like twenty years, not four. And the growth was probably more emotional than academic. I began to see myself as someone who could succeed. I was no longer a failure. I have to give a great deal of credit for this growth to my high school resource-room teacher.

Until high school I hated reading. I really hated it! Then I took a literature course and I read *Appoinment in Samara*, by John O'Hara. What a wonderful book! It was the first time I got everything from the text. That is, I recognized all the symbolism. I began to read a lot after that. In fact, I minored in literature in college. I read all the time now. My books are my trophies. I love going to old bookstores and collecting books.

I feel I have come a tremendous way. I try to look at each of my failures as a door of opportunity. But sometimes the struggle and the memory of the struggle creep up on me. I believe the support of teachers and other significant people have contributed most to my success. A lot of small successes and positive feedback had an enormous impact. I now view my life as a continual series of learning experiences. Learning is an adventure, no longer a chore.

I am often hard on myself; I want to do everything perfectly, but I know I can help others celebrate small successes.

When I can no longer make others feel good, I will have to find something else to do with my life. I have a few principles to guide my teaching. Teachers need to figure out how children learn. Failure is opportunity. Love is the most important teaching technique. I believe if all teachers adopted such principles, they would preserve the emotional health of the children they teach.

A Learning Disabled Woman Succeeds in College

Molly Sumner

When Molly Sumner was in grade school, she was diagnosed with dyslexia, auditory processing disorders, and attention deficit disorder. According to national statistics, her odds of graduating from college were very slim. But Sumner succeeded. In the following excerpt, she recounts the ways in which her learning experiences were shaped by schools that offered alternative instructional techniques and how she thrived in this atmosphere. To her and other students like her, this meant the freedom to work outside the norm.

My early school experiences? They were really hard. I didn't read very well, I felt alienated from a lot of my classmates, and my teachers weren't all that helpful. For example, they'd try and move me to the front of the class or have me sit next to a really smart kid, in the hope that somehow—suppose through osmosis—I would start to learn. All it did, though, was make me feel humiliated, because I'd just end up wondering why everyone else was doing so well and I was doing so poorly.

Around second or third grade, my parents and my teachers began to suspect I might have a learning disability. I remember I had to take a lot of different tests and was eventually diagnosed with LD [a learning disability], though being diagnosed didn't seem to make a whole lot of difference, at least while I was in public school. The attitude seemed to be: "Okay, you have learning disabilities, we're going to stick you in a special ed classroom for two or three hours a day so you can get help with your class work." And my feeling was: "Hey, you're only helping me get it done, you're not really helping me to understand it any better." The whole thing started to seem like a joke.

My mom finally pulled me out of school in the fifth grade and homeschooled me. She had to battle with the school system, and she had to work really hard to fulfill all the requirements. But she wrote out the lesson plan and did all the things she needed to do. And homeschooling worked out for a while, but it ended up being very lonely. We tried getting together with some homeschooling groups, but these were kids who'd been homeschooled their entire lives, and I didn't feel like I fit in very well. They all knew each other, and I ended up feeling like a new kid who had just moved into the neighborhood. A lot of the homeschooling organizations are also very religious, and I don't come from a particularly religious family, so that also made things kind of uncomfortable.

The Right School Makes All the Difference

Finally, my mom pushed hard and got me into the Craig School, a private school that specializes in students with learning disabilities. And there was a teacher there, Mrs. Okey, who was just *stupendous*. She got me into reading, she got me to love books and she really taught me how to read again. I found out that I loved fantasy novels, and suddenly I couldn't get my hands on enough of them. In the fifth grade I had been reading at barely a third grade level, and with Mrs. Okey I jumped three or four reading levels in one year. It was challenging, but something just clicked for me when I was in her class. We all really enjoyed the books we were reading; we'd all be really excited to find out what happened next, and we were all reading at the same pace.

We read some difficult books, too. Mary Shelly's *Franken-stein*, [William] Golding's *Lord of the Flies, The Yearling*, by Marjorie Rawlings. When we read *The Yearling*, it was especially great because Mrs. Okey was from the South, and she was there to explain a lot of the language. We also played around with some of the books. Everybody would pick a character, and then you'd read just that character's dialogue out loud, and the teacher would read the non-dialogue narration. It wasn't like we were reading a book, we were learning a story, learning about the ideas the book was trying to put across. And we were never afraid to not understand something—either somebody would know the answer or we'd all work together and figure it out.

Unfortunately, the Craig School only went through eighth grade. I went to a Catholic school, Baily Ellard, for about six months; then the Center School, which had a lot of kids with emotional problems and I really didn't feel safe; and then back to a mainstream school. My mom was desperate to find me another high school, someplace where I wouldn't need to leave again after six months. And we finally found the Sage Day School, a really nice school in Rochelle Park.

It was a long commute every morning, but it was worth it. I made a lot of friends, and I really learned. They had open classrooms, you were given a lot of freedom. With math, I finished my algebra II book and started on trig and calculus. Something just clicked for me, and I learned a lot of it on my own. With science, I could sit in class and have a discussion with the teacher—they really wanted to hear that you wanted to learn. The classes were small and everyone had time for you. There were a lot of extracurricular activities, and I ended up graduating from there with a 4.0.

Next Step—College

I'd always wanted to go to college. I was of the mindset that it was what you did after you got out of high school. And I wanted to learn so much more, but unfortunately my SATs stank. I applied to three colleges—Rutgers, Ursinus and Drew. Drew was my first choice and I was lucky because that was the college I got into. Tom Kean, the former New Jersey governor, is the president of Drew, and when I was at the Craig School we had a letter from him that was framed and hanging on the wall. In the letter, he wrote that he had learning disabilities too, that he had gotten through them, and that we could too. It was very inspiring for me and it made me feel like: "Yeah, we're not these stupid kids that everybody makes us out to be. I can succeed too."

I lived on campus, even though Drew was close to my home. The college was very accommodating, and some of the professors really bent over backwards for me. The first year was really kinda scary, though. It was all in my hands—I had to get myself up and get to class on time, and they're at all these different hours instead of the regular 8 to 3. It was all about, "I have to remember to go to class; I have to have my books ready; I have to have the right state of mind." The classes were longer than what I'd been used to and I didn't know how to take notes. Kids with LD generally aren't expected to go to college and, as a result, we don't get taught a lot of college skills.

And then I'd find out that I'd have a 10-page paper due! That was more than a little bit intimidating! Or I'd find out that I had to cover 200 pages of reading in a week. But I could go up to my professors and tell them what was wrong, and they would almost always accommodate me. Like they'd tell me that the most important part of the reading was in these particular chapters and to focus on those. Or they'd give me extra time. Some of them might say, "Well, you gotta read it," and I'd try my best and if I couldn't answer every question in class, they'd understand.

But my professors and I agreed that my reading was holding me back. So my second year the school hooked me up with software from Kurzweil that scanned the material and could read it back to me. And it really caught me up in my reading—after about half way through my third year, I didn't need to use it any more. In fact, by my senior year, I'd become so used to college life that I did 90% of the work without accommodations. Maybe a little extra time here and there, but that was all.

Finding Motivation

And even though it was tough, knowing that Tom Kean had LD gave me a lot of hope; it was like, "Well, if he can do it, I can do it." And my mom and my friends were all really positive and really supportive too and helped keep me from giving up. But I could be my own worst enemy and my own worst critic, and let myself believe I couldn't accomplish something that deep down I knew I could do, because I was either scared or intimidated.

But I loved the atmosphere—that really helped to get me through it. I just loved that there was all this stuff to learn. I loved the lecture classes, and I loved the small discussion classes even more. There was a whole series of religion seminars I took, and we'd just sit and learn about so many great things and great thoughts. I loved the faculty and the friends I made there, and I also just loved the way the campus looked. If I was having a bad day in my room, I could get out and go for a walk and that would make all the difference.

My plans for the future have kind of bounced around, but right now I'm looking into starting my own business, a pet store. I love the pet industry and the pet trade—animals are my thing and I love working with them. There are so many amazing creatures out there that people can have as companions, but there are a lot of things people don't understand about animals. I want to make sure people know enough so that they and the animals will both do well together. I would really love to have my own store, though I don't have the financial backing right now, so I'll have to wait.

For anyone with LD who wants to go to college, you can do it if you have the right kind of support. I count myself lucky, because I got the support I needed and having it was critical for me. But if you have that support from friends and family, you can get through college if you really try—it will be tough, but you'll be very proud of yourself in the end.

Learning Despite Learning Disabilities

Dale S. Brown

Dale S. Brown considers her learning disabilities serious. When she writes about them, she lists them as "perceptual problems including visual, auditory, and motor modalities. My difficulties involve sequencing, discrimination, and figure ground tasks. I also have a directional handicap and slight motor problems."

Brown is the author of several books on learning disabilities and has specialized in the field of employment and equality for those with learning disabilities. In the following article, she describes her experiences as a college student, first at Pitzer College—with mixed results—then flourishing after transferring to the less traditional Antioch College.

I decided to take easy classes my first quarter, since social adjustment was my most important task. Immediately, Antioch [College] made me feel at home. The first night there, Lynn, my roommate, arrived. We talked for hours. Clearly we were on our way to a friendship.

In the morning, we met Eileen, a woman across the hall. On our way to breakfast, several residents of our hall joined us. As we were eating, Lynn said, "You know, Dale, it's funny, but it was easier talking to you last night. Your staring is bugging me."

"It bugs me too," said Eileen. "Is something wrong with your eyes?"

"I think so," I replied. "But, I don't know what's wrong with them."

"Well, lot's of people stare," said Mark. "It doesn't bother me at all."

Dale S. Brown, "Learning Despite Learning Disabilities," *Helping the Learning-Disabled Student*, edited by Marlin R. Schmidt, and Hazel Z. Sprandel, San Francisco: Jossey-Bass, 1982. Reproduced by permission of the author.

"Well, you're not sitting right across from her," replied Lynn. "I feel like she's looking right through me."

The conversation moved on to other things. It took me awhile to absorb the feedback, but at Antioch I began to understand why I made people uneasy. The "mark of the outcast" was real, but I could control it. I became conscious of moving my eyes and not letting them stare at a person or an object.

At Antioch, feedback was frequently given, requested, and received. Many students had been through encounter, sensitivity, and other forms of therapy. Through listening to the comments of my peers, I learned that certain aspects of my appearance made it difficult for others to relate to me. I tilted my head slightly. In order to look at something, I often moved my head and entire body instead of my eyes. To repress my hyperactivity, I held my muscles rigid. I was often startled and would make sudden movements. These were the visible signs of the dysfunction of my central nervous system. They were not obvious, yet people registered them in their subconscious mind. They often said they could feel a "strong aura", a "force field" around me. Students told me that I "tried too hard" and "looked nervous." During my years at college, I learned to control my body. This helped me make a good first impression.

Real Learning Begins

Classes at Antioch were very different from the classes at Pitzer [College]. In my printing class, the teacher announced, "I am here as a resource. Everyone is expected to turn in a printed project at the end of the quarter. But I won't be teaching you. Just ask questions if you need help with your project."

A student shyly asked, "Do you have any guidelines for this project?"

"No," he replied, "except it should be longer than one line."

An upperclass student took charge and requested that the teacher name each machine in the room, tell us the order in which they were used, and demonstrate the functioning of the light table. I asked if there were any instruction books for the machine. The teacher said "No," but several of my classmates looked at me with respect.

The unstructured educational approach at Antioch did not work for everyone. The dropout rate was high. It was rumored that some students graduated without having done any work. However, Antioch was effective for me, and I began to enjoy my studies. Now that I didn't have to fear failure, it was possible to attempt difficult classes. For example, I took Spanish again and passed it. I got organized and wrote out my schedule each day. The first few days of each quarter were spent practicing the route from class to class, from dormitory to class, and from lunchroom to class. My attendance became close to perfect. I liked small classes, so I took the ones that met early in the morning and tended to have less students.

Antioch assumed that everyone learned differently. I never felt handicapped or special. For the first part of my school career, I didn't know I had learning disabilities. Yet, at my request, faculty made accommodations for me:

1. It took me longer to complete my work, so I would always ask permission to turn in one paper or project late. Unless there was a good reason not to, this request was granted. The communications department allowed me to practice with the equipment for longer amounts of time than was needed by other students.

2. Papers and projects could be substituted for taking examinations.

3. Remedial classes were not labeled negatively. In a writing workshop, I wrote a paper each week and met with a teacher who helped me with structure and grammar. Students competed to get into this class. They had to be interviewed and

show motivation. I was proud to get in, not ashamed of taking it. Antioch also offered a math workshop and a science workshop.

4. When asked, faculty helped students. I frequently approached professors for help with difficult material. They were generous with their time, always checked extra work that was handed in, and often complimented my efforts.

Course work was still a struggle, but it was manageable. Classes were smaller and more social. Discussion was more common than lecture. Often the whole group worked together to complete a project such as making a film, building something for the campus, putting on radio programs, or writing a paper. On any project, there was always the option of working with someone else.

Social Skills Develop

In this way, my social skills developed as an integral part of my academic work. Social skills and class material were thought about in the same analytic way. For example, I remember talking to someone when we were both standing on the library steps. At one point in the conversation, she stepped down one step and leaned slightly away from me. "That means she wants to end the conversation," I thought and drew my comments to a close.

I watched people, analyzed what they were doing, imitated their behavior, and watched how people reacted to me. I learned how to time my comments in a group so that I didn't interrupt. Joining conversations became easier. I discovered the importance of making eye contact before beginning a conversation. I practiced "leader" and "follower" body language. My academic success and problem solving skills helped me. I became more confident and accepted rejections more philosophically.

My social development was enhanced by the work-study program. Students studied for three months, worked for three months, studied for six months, worked for six months, studied for three months and repeated the cycle. Jobs could be found anywhere. The constant variation in peer groups helped me. I never established an eccentric reputation, and I could consistently improve.

My learning disabilities caused me problems on the job. In a factory, while working on an assembly line, my production was low because of my poor coordination. In a Montessori school, I had difficulty learning to use the preschool equipment which required perceptual-motor abilities. Filling out forms and following directions were difficulties in all of my jobs. However, I was usually successful. In a large institution for retarded children, 70 percent of the children met treatment goals which staff had warned me were too ambitious. When I taught English in Colombia, South America, my students did well, and I enjoyed teaching. Even in the factory, my work on an employees' committee resulted in several positive changes in working conditions.

Discovering My Learning Disabilities

One of the most important moments in my college career was when I realized I had learning disabilities. I saw a counselor about my work-related problems. She told me it sounded as if I had perceptual problems and instructed me to go to the library and find out about learning disabilities.

When I realized I had a handicap, I knew the problems I had been struggling with were real. In comparison with the learning disabled people who were described in the books, I had done quite well. I became proud of my academic success rather than ashamed of my long hours of study. I felt clever about coming to campus early to practice the routes to and from classes. My need to analyze the "social code" made sense. Up until that point, I thought my unconscious mind was making me feel distant from other people. Now I knew I was fighting a perceptual problem, and as my self-image became stronger, I became more understanding of my failures.

I had always felt different from everyone else. Now, I knew why. I was different, but in a specific way. My understanding of that difference ended my fundamental loneliness. Now it was possible to be open to the similarities between me and other people.

It wasn't easy emotionally to accept this new information. I had to go through stages of self-pity and anger at people who had hurt me in the past. It was clear that I had to learn more about my own handicaps before I could help children with handicaps, and I changed my major from special education to communications. I learned how to use video equipment, make a film and to work in a radio station.

For the next few years, I continued to work hard. Knowledge of my specific areas of weakness made me more efficient while studying. My coping skills were reevaluated. For example, once I realized that my hearing was inaccurate, I learned to relax while listening to people. When following instructions, I was careful to remember the first and second commands. I often asked several people to teach me the same material so none of them would get impatient. I always wrote down what was important to know. I also accepted my limitations. My last four classes at Antioch were divided so that I only took two per quarter. This gave me time to learn the material thoroughly.

Receiving my diploma was one of the proudest moments of my life. After the students graduated, we had to say our goodbyes. Males and females alike were crying and hugging each other. As I hugged my friends, I clung to them not wanting to leave the community that college had formed, where we had strengthened each other. But eventually I let go. Antioch had taught me how to work, how to learn, and how to be part of a community larger than myself. I was ready to face the next phase of my life.

CHAPTER 5

Learning Disabilities
in the Workplace

Overwhelming Challenges at Work

Samantha Abeel

Dealing with undiagnosed dyscalculia, Samantha Abeel couldn't keep up with many of her classes and found time management nearly impossible. After the discovery of her learning disorder, she took special education classes, and with the support of her family, she graduated from high school and was accepted to Mount Holyoke College.

During the summer before her freshman year at Mount Holyoke, Abeel worked in a local restaurant and in a hotel, experiences she relates in the following excerpt from her memoir, My Thirteenth Winter. *Her frustrations at work echo those of many learning disabled individuals. Abeel has met with other successes, however, publishing the book,* Reach for the Moon *when she was fifteen, graduating from Mount Holyoke with honors, and serving as a residence hall counselor at Interlochen Center for the Arts in Michigan.*

After graduation, it was time for me to begin looking for a summer job. A family friend for whom I had often babysat owned an upscale restaurant, a favorite of the wealthy summer crowd, and offered me a job as a busser.

I would have to prove myself, he said, but within the first couple of weeks I should make tip pool (meaning I would share in the pooled tips of the waitstaff) and be able to gather together a significant amount of money to put toward college. Little did I know that it would be an absolute disaster.

A Typical Night at the Restaurant

I arrived at the restaurant early, anxious about time and not sure how long it will take me to get there. As usual, I have already completed the tasks the two table bussers on duty are expected to complete before the doors open for the evening. I have thoroughly cleaned both bathrooms and vacuumed beneath the tables and chairs in the dining room. I take satisfaction in completing these tasks, scrubbing the white porcelain of the toilet bowl, washing the sink, and hearing the gritty crackle as the vacuum sucks up tiny particles of sand and crumbs from the gray carpet. These are jobs I feel I have mastered. I can do them without fault. Knowing this helps to alleviate my guilt for all the tasks I will do wrong tonight while carrying out my normal duties as a busser.

I help two of the servers smooth the pressed white tablecloths over the square surfaces of the tables, and I make my way about the room, lighting the tea candles in their clear glass holders, a hint of sulfur and a trail of wavering reflecting flames in my wake. This part always feels as if a stage is being set.

I finish tying on the final item of my uniform, a white, knee-length apron. Now, all that is left is to wait for the first customers to come through the front doors. I feel nothing but dread and nervous tension. I do my best to block out and ignore the faintly disappointed looks of the servers when they see that I am on duty. I try to forget that it's halfway through the summer and I still haven't been placed on tip pool, while every other busser, most younger than me, has. I am barely making enough money to justify the gas to get to the restaurant, let alone enough to put aside for college expenses.

The night is a busy one, every table full. I move quickly to reset a table but I forget the salt and pepper shakers. As I reach to get them, the server I am working with moves by and mumbles that four tables need water. I go for the pitcher of water and I am stopped by the hostess who tells me that I reversed where the knives and spoons should be placed on the last table I set, and she had to move them herself after she had seated the customers. I barely feel guilty or apologetic anymore, just numb. I begin to refill water glasses. When I finish, I help to clear a table of four, bending at the knees to get under the heavy tray. Then I am asked to make more coffee.

I take the tray in and stand in front of the machine, a jumble of instructions running through my head. I awkwardly complete the task as best as my muddled mind will allow, then hurry to carry out a tray of dinners for another server. I go to get the water pitcher again and am stopped by a server who asks if I was the one who made coffee last, because someone forgot to put a filter in the machine and it has leaked all over the kitchen. She doesn't give me time to respond. No need. She has already angrily pushed her way back into the kitchen to make a new pot. Tears well up and sting the bottom of my eyelids. I push them back, telling myself I will just have to ask someone to help me with the machine next time, not dwelling on the fact that this will be my fifth coffee screwup in the last two weeks.

Why Can't I Do That?

The other busser moves along with the traffic impeccably. She silently and quickly carries out her tasks, filling water, assisting staff, anticipating what they will need before they even have to ask for it. I hear her complimented by the hostess and other staff, and I am envious of her cool composure and ease. I am amazed at how she keeps it all straight, remembering all the steps in order, her speed and efficiency. I fall so short. I want nothing more than to please, but can't seem to. Instead, I have three tables to reset, two parties waiting at the door, and no time for me to accomplish any of it. Meanwhile, the hostess has to fill water glasses at two of my tables, and another server has to help bring tea to my table when she should be taking orders at her own.

The night finally ends, and I drive home around midnight. I walk in through the back door and answer the sleepy voice of my mother who always asks, "Is that you?"

"Yes," I whisper back. I climb the stairs, my feet aching, and relish the relief of taking off my shoes and untucking my shirt. I crawl into bed, but don't fall asleep. Instead, I find myself reliving the night, processing it like a videotape in my mind. Every mess-up, every mistake, runs through my head again and again as I try to figure out what went wrong, try desperately to make it right, try to remember how to do it better next time. I toss and turn, the pace of the restaurant staying with me long after the tea lights have burned themselves out, and the last half-empty coffee cups and wine glasses have been cleared for the night. I try to forget that I have to go back again tomorrow.

Another Job, Same Frustrations

Desperate for money to help pay for school, I was forced to take another job that wouldn't conflict with my night job and wouldn't require that I work a cash register or deal with numbers. After frantically looking, and being turned down because most places had already done their hiring for the summer, I finally got a job at one of the hotels in town, cleaning rooms.

Working at the Hotel

In the hotel room, MTV blares on the television. I can hear it over the noise of the vacuum as I kneel on all fours and wipe down the tile-lined floor with a clean rag in an attempt to remove every last hair. In the other room, I hear the vacuum roar cut off abruptly as Pat pulls the plug from the wall and begins to coil it around the back of the machine. Its wheels squawk as she drags it out to the cleaning cart in the hallway. Pat is in a hurry today. She has a date tonight with a trucker she met at the Shell station where she works nights. She is one of the five full-time cleaning women at the hotel, and has been for five years.

We have been working full speed since early morning and have agreed to go without lunch in order to finish the five rooms we have left. Two of the rooms on our list are suites that have endless miles of porcelain to wipe down and two king-sized beds with two very heavy, very wide king-sized mattresses to lift and tuck and walk around.

I work here from 7:30 A.M. until 3:00 or 4:00 P.M. and then I run home, take a shower, and leave for work at the restaurant at 5:00 P.M. Even though there are some days where my schedule isn't doubled up so I work both jobs, it has been a grueling schedule to keep. But I need the money.

The Difficulties Abound

I find that even though I am performing tasks I have done a million times over, I still have to give this job my full concentration. In fact, I struggle every day with simple things, like remembering to leave soap in the bathroom or leaving the right number of towels. Sometimes I forget a step, like dusting or taking out the garbage. My brain constantly feels scrambled. Already today, I have forgotten to put trash liners in one room and to wipe off the balcony furniture in another. I can hear Pat heave a heavy sigh and shake her head at me, as our supervisor makes the round of this last room and finds that I failed to replace the towels.

I grab the forgotten towels from the cart and quickly walk back to the room while Pat pushes on ahead down the hall. I feel my temperature rise and a wave of frustration wash over me. Why can't I do it right? Between this job and the restaurant, I am beginning to feel like I am buried under a heavy weight that I can't seem to crawl out from. No matter how hard I try, I can't get it right. I feel like a failure.

Depression and Self-Doubt

Midway through the summer. I sank into a deep depression. I didn't smile anymore. I didn't laugh. Nothing seemed funny. I felt worthless, drained, inferior. No matter what I did, it seemed I did it wrong. Life was an arduous, exhausting task that I had to get up and endure—not something to be lived or enjoyed.

I wondered, *What is this roller-coaster ride I am on? When will it end? Why can't I just be normal? Why does everything have to be so hard?* And now I was going to go off to college and live on my own when I was still afraid of driving myself somewhere alone. I slipped toward despair.

What Am I Going to Do?

Mom and I sit in the van, which is parked overlooking the wide curve of the bay. The late August sky is gray and heavy with clouds that hang dramatically over the turbulent gray water, and whitecaps whip up with the strong northwesterly wind. I leave in a week for college.

She is worried about me and knows the two jobs I worked this summer were hard. She notices that I am silent more often and I smile less. I don't seem myself. She tries to reassure me and remind me of the things I do well, such as the speaking I did this past year, or the sets I built for the musical. She reflects that the negative restaurant experience was mostly the owner's fault—and my learning difference; that I was really good at babysitting. She sounds convincing; perhaps she is trying to persuade herself as well as me. But the heavy weight just hangs here, making it hard for me to breathe.

I stare out over the wide stretch of water and sky, at the beautifully tilted curves of land that heave alongside the shore. I feel so defeated, so numb. No matter how many times I am reminded that I am about to attend a prestigious college, or that I had a book published, or have given keynote presentations at national conferences, it doesn't matter. I still feel inadequate. It doesn't matter that I had successfully stage-managed a musical that year or had won awards at my high school. All that matters are the knife, fork, and spoon—the pieces of silverware I couldn't remember where to place. The simple steps

I couldn't carry out to make coffee; the forgotten bars of soap and trash can liners; alway feeling like more of a hindrance than a help. I ask my mother as hot tears run down my face, "What am I going to do if I can't even bus a table or clean a hotel room?"

Lessons from a Hyperactive Dyslexic

Paul Orfalea and Ann Marsh

Paul Orfalea founded Kinko's copy business in 1970 and retired from the business in 2000. He now teaches college business courses and lectures to professionals nationwide. Diagnosed with dyslexia and attention deficit hyperactivity disorder (conditions which Orfalea calls "learning opportunities" rather than learning disabilities), he faced many obstacles in his career. Orfalea's strategic philosophy is captured in his observation that: "There isn't a machine at Kinko's I can operate. I could barely run the first copier we leased back in 1970. It didn't matter. All I knew was that I could sell what came out of it." As he explains in the following excerpt from his autobiography, Copy This! Lessons from a Hyperactive Dyslexic Who Turned a Bright Idea into One of America's Best Companies, *he found that his challenges made him open to innovative ideas and to tapping the talents of his employees—concepts that made Kinko's wildly profitable.*

Not many kids manage to flunk the second grade, but I did. I couldn't learn the alphabet. This code called reading, so easy for other students, I found difficult to break. They read as though angels whispered into their ears. They wrote in graceful curves and perfectly straight lines. I made chicken scratches. To me, a sentence was a road map with ink stains in all the critical places.

Consequently, I became a goof-off. Of the eight schools my parents enrolled me in, four expelled me. In third grade, my frustrated teachers sent me to a school for "mentally retarded" kids, housed in a teacher's residence in Hollywood.

Most of my classmates suffered from Down's syndrome or other conditions of severe mental and physical impairment. Fortunately, I was given an IQ test, scored 130, and rejoined the public school system. Still, things didn't get much better. I may not have been able to read, but I could find my way to the principal's office blindfolded. My typical report card came back with two C's, three D's, and an F. A brilliant tutor named Selma Herr finally managed to teach me to read, after a fashion, using phonics. I graduated from high school, with a focus in wood shop, eighth from the bottom of my class of 1,200. Frankly, I still have no idea how those seven kids managed to do worse than I did.

My name is Paul Orfalea (OR-fah-la). In 1970, I started a copy shop in Santa Barbara, California, in an 8-foot by 12-foot storefront next to a hamburger stand. I called it Kinko's after the nickname college friends gave me because of my kinky hair. Today, there are more than 1,200 Kinko's locations across the globe. The revenues from those stores top $2 billion annually. Federal Express, our former vendor and the new owner of Kinko's, plans to dramatically increase the number of retail outlets. I am most proud of the fact that, before I retired, *Fortune* named Kinko's one of the best places to work in the country three times in a row. More than 100 of my earliest coworkers and partners are millionaires today because of what we built together at Kinko's. As someone with a condition I now know is called "dyslexia," I could have never predicted I would make my name in what is essentially the "reading business." Kinko's is not only a fixture on downtown street corners, but a fixture in the minds of millions of customers who use it to solve any number of their problems.

Teaching People to Relate

Today, I spend most Mondays in an unusual spot for someone with my skill set. I'm back in Santa Barbara, not far from that first Kinko's, teaching economics to college seniors at the University of California at Santa Barbara. Naturally, I use a different teaching strategy than other teachers. I don't use a roster to take roll. I take Polaroids of each student on the first day and scrawl their first names on each one. I keep this stack of photos in my pocket and shuffle through it when I need to. When I ask them for writing assignments (which is rarely), I never want more than one single page of clear and concise prose. I could care less about their grades. (I give almost all of them A's.) Instead, I teach them skills that have little to do with academics or test scores. Among other things, I teach them new ways to think about money and investing, how to present their ideas verbally, how to talk with people from "authority figures" to each other. To this end, I run an exercise to teach them one of the hardest things in the world to learn— harder than calculus, harder than economic theory, harder than fixing a photocopier.

"Peter," I say, picking a student at random. "Isn't there a lovely young woman in this class who you'd like to ask out for Wednesday night?" Nervous laughter spreads across the room. People start looking at each other or down at their shoes. They're thinking, "*This* is a world economics class?" Yes, it is.

"You want me to just *ask somebody out?*" Peter asks, incredulous. We've gotten to know each other over the past couple of classes. Now he looks at me as though I've gone insane. I am accustomed to getting this sort of reaction in life. I give him back an equally incredulous look. "You mean you wouldn't *want* to go out with one of these lovely ladies? Peter, this is your chance."

"OK," Peter says looking across at Wendy. With a toss of the head, he says, "Hey, what are you doing Wednesday night?" Verrry cool.

"No, no, no!" I say. I wave my hands in the air like a conductor. "Ask her nicely, nicely. Be polite." Have you ever noticed that kids these days really don't know how to talk to each other? Peter begins again. He sits up a little straighter. He looks her in the eye.

"Wendy," he begins, making eye contact. "Would-you-like-to-go-out-with-me-Wednesday-night?" This is a different kid entirely, both polite and courageous.

Now Wendy is embarrassed. It turns out she has a boyfriend! I ask her if she knows what she's passing up. She murmurs something and looks down. But Peter isn't off the hook. I get him to ask somebody else. This time Carol, shyly, says yes. I pull out a crumpled wad of bills from my pocket and give Peter some money, because most college kids are always pretty poor.

"Where are you gonna go?" I ask him. He hasn't thought this far ahead. "Maybe Palazzio?" he ventures. "Oh, that's a great place," I tell him. I get this pair to settle on the hour they will meet on Wednesday. By this time, there's a lot of laughter. Believe me, no one is bored. "Seven P.M.?" I confirm. "Great, maybe I'll come," I say. "I'll see you there."

Knowing We Need Others

I've never turned up, but I like them to think I might. Next week, I find out how the date went. Maybe I get another pair or two in class set up on dates. Sometimes the students keep dating each other, sometimes they don't. But the point is, they get a chance to learn how to talk to each other. They get to see someone navigate rejection and survive it. They get to see someone asking for something he wants or needs from another person. Sometimes that's all we need to learn to do in life.

The truth is that most of the boys are dying to ask out one of the girls. And most of the girls have an eye on one of the boys. Even if they're straight-A students, speed readers, and star athletes, they're scared half to death of putting themselves on the line. They need a push. This is one of the greatest lessons I learned from my own struggles, from my dyslexia, my restlessness, and what others call my ADHD or "attention deficit/hyperactivity disorder." (I dislike using the term "deficit"; I don't think it is one.) Doing life alone is not second best, it's impossible. We need other people. We need to know how to talk with them, argue with them, build with them, and introduce ourselves to them. We need a push. It's funny to think that human beings forget this fact, especially the straight-A types.

At Kinko's I was a tireless matchmaker among the ranks of our coworkers. I constantly urged people to fall in love and marry each other. I believed in it and I still do! Hundreds of our partners, managers, and coworkers were married to each other. I'm very proud of the fact that, at one point before I left the company, I discovered that among our 200 top people we had only seven divorces. Many of our customers used Kinko's as a dating service, as well. Thousands of them got married after meeting each other over our copy machines. Kinko's was similar to another people-oriented company I admire, Southwest Airlines, which counts more than 1,000 married couples among its 34,000 coworkers. That's a great statistic. I knew our coworkers would be stronger in teams than on their own. It's possible to go all the way through your schooling years without learning this. Given the cards I drew at birth, I never had the chance to forget, not even for a moment.

The Benefits of Thinking Differently

This is only one of the many gifts of my "disorders," all of which contributed enormously to the building of both Kinko's and of my life. They propelled me to think differently. They forced me to rely on other people. I was prevented from taking inspiration from books; I had to learn from the world itself, directly. I had to rely on my own eyes, a skill not enough people make use of these days. My "disabilities" enabled me to focus on the big picture at Kinko's, something I call being "on" your business instead of "in" it. My friend Tom O'Malia, former head of the Center for the Study of Entrepreneurship at the University of Southern California, taught me this concept. He told me that too many people are mired in the details of their lives. They are stuck down "in" their lives, rather than staying "on" them. They miss the larger picture; they don't face the uncomfortable questions that, once posed, can force dramatic and necessary change. My dad had a saying for this. He would tell me, "The mundane is like a cancer." He meant that all the busywork of your life prevents you from actually living.

Taking Care of Business

Running a company in a world full of readers was . . . well, an interesting experience. I certainly didn't behave like other executives. If you opened the drawers and filing cabinets of my office, you would have seen . . . nothing. I didn't keep paperwork, files, a pen, or a computer. What for? As a nonreader, I wouldn't be using them much. In a way, the office was just for show because I didn't like spending time there. I didn't like sitting around and reading long, novelistic reports. I didn't get caught up in the minutiae of meeting minutes. (I'd rather stick pins in my eyes than sit through a board meeting.) Coworkers helped with my written correspondence. I was so avid about staying "on" my business that I was maniacal—fanatical!—about responding to my mail the same day I got it. My longtime colleague CiCie Frederickson learned to write my letters based on our brief conversations. "You figure out how to say it," I'd tell her. Later, her husband, Dan Frederickson, the president of Kinko's, also helped write correspondence for me, too. My office was empty because I had an In Box and an Out Box—but no storage box in between. I took care of business the same day it landed on my desk.

Though I couldn't avoid some writing, most vital communications were transmitted verbally, by voice mail, or in person. When I was with Kinko's, we were an oral company, a verbal company. My restlessness propelled me out of doors.

How many managers do you know who *really* understand what is happening at the frontlines of their business? I did. I visited stores to find out what our different locations were doing right. Anybody can sit around in an office thinking about what people are doing wrong. My job was to get out and find out what people were doing right—and exploit it. Then, I tried to spread those practices throughout the Kinko's network.

My high school degree in wood shop belies the fact that I also have no mechanical ability to speak of. There isn't a machine at Kinko's I can operate. I could barely run the first copier we leased back in 1970. It didn't matter. All I knew was that I could sell what came out of it. From day one at Kinko's I relied on others to operate those machines, to run the store, to come up with groundbreaking new ideas, to expand our business, and to keep me and everybody else constantly inspired. The same is true today. I rely on others to run our real estate ventures, our investments, and our philanthropic endeavors. You're right if you're wondering whether or not I *wrote* these words you're reading. As with every other undertaking in my life, I relied on someone else—in this case, my coauthor Ann Marsh. Too many people think they have to do life on their own, but I've found the best way to live is to share the burdens, as well as the joys, with others. My motto has always been "Anybody else can do it better."

The Problem with Labels

These days, people are quick to label others with terms like "learning disabled," ADHD, ADD, "dyslexic," and a host of other maladies. Kids often come up to me and say, "I *am* ADHD," as opposed to, "I *have* ADHD." What does that do to their self-esteem? Drugs like Ritalin and Prozac are prescribed as quick fixes. I am not against those drugs. In fact, my life improved dramatically once I started taking Prozac a couple of years back. But, before giving drugs to our kids, we need to better understand what they are trying to erase: the highly varied ways people think and process information. How many innovators, I wonder, are lost to us simply because their talents and skills cannot be accurately perceived or measured? And why are we so hung up on measuring everyone, anyway? The very bedevilment we are so eager to cure in a person may hold the key to his genius. I speak regularly to adults, kids, budding entrepreneurs, parents, business students, corporate executives, and academics and, believe me, the things I tell them are not what they learn in classrooms. When tearful parents come up to me to talk about their child's "learning disorder," I ask them, "Oh, you mean his learning *opportunity*? What is your child good at? What does he like to do?" When I meet their kids, I tell them, "You are blessed." It is easy to forget that part of the equation in the face of a dire-sounding prognosis.

In Good Company

I didn't know it at the time I opened the first Kinko's, but there is a long history of innovators and achievers who owe their particular brilliance, at least in part, to their "deficits." This is a little appreciated fact, but those with learning opportunities, and even people with mood disorders, make up the ranks of some of the most successful and inventive members of our society. They have for millennia. Some speculate that Leonardo da Vinci, Winston Churchill, Albert Einstein, and Walt Disney were dyslexic, though there's no way to say for certain. A *Fortune* cover story, "The Dyslexic CEO," featured the startling number of successful businesspeople with dyslexia, from Virgin Record's founder Richard Branson and telecom pioneer Craig McCaw to Cisco CEO John Chambers and celebrated trial attorney David Boies to discount brokerage founder Charles Schwab. Add to that list IKEA founder Ingvar Kamprad, whose fortune *Forbes* estimates at $18.5 billion. I'm in good company. All of these innovators survived an educational system determined to make them feel like failures. We are the lucky ones. Some think our penal system is crammed with wayward visionaries who never found the support they needed to make the capitalist system work for them. Some of my closest friends in high school and college were social outcasts. Some of them did end up in jail. I could relate to them all.

Fortunately, my racing, jumping mind, my inability to sit still, my difficulty reading—all of these qualities led me to develop what other people call an unorthodox, people-centered, big-picture business model. To a peddler like me it's simply what came naturally. In this model, when all systems are go, businessmen and women value customers and each other, understand the importance of cash flow, liquidity, savings, and risk taking. They cut quickly through red tape (because there isn't any), grow rapidly without losing perspective, and surround themselves with the right people. To this day, Kinko's (now FedEx Kinko's) is one of only a very few competitors from that original field of mom-and-pop copy shops that has survived to become a multinational. FedEx Kinko's is now the dominant retail document management chain in the world. As we grew, we continued to insist on respecting every single one of our (at the time) 25,000 coworkers for their unique contributions. We created a unique company with a unique culture. The fact that *Fortune* repeatedly named it one of the best places to work is due, in no small part, to the fact that I understood that anybody else really *could* do it better.

Differences Can Be Advantages in the Workplace

Donald A. Winkler

An undeniable corporate success, Donald A. Winkler is not only a powerful executive, but also a national spokesman for learning disabilities. In the following essay, he confesses to his own limitations, shows how they give him the capacity to think creatively, and offers suggestions for techniques that will make life easier for those with learning disabilities.

I walk into a room, crowded with people, all looking at me with expectant faces. They are 500 Ford Credit employees gathered from around the world, waiting to hear the words of their new Chairman and CEO. My introduction is given, and our employees are told that today Ford Credit has 9 million customers, 11,500 dealers, $1.26 billion in profits, 19,000 employees, 290 offices around the world and $15.5 billion in assets. The audience waits to hear what I will say. I walk to the podium thinking, these people probably believe that I must be so smart, capable and confident to be in this position. They do not know the steps that I have taken to be walking there.

The reality is that I work harder than most people. The reality is that I am using a variety of compensation mechanisms to help me deal with dyslexia and a series of learning differences that make it difficult for me to concentrate, make it difficult for me to read and handle numbers, and make it difficult for me to visualize normal every day things. The reality also is that with the support of family, friends and teachers, I have taken what could have been an insecure life, filled with self-doubt and minimal personal and professional success and turned it around to contribute to the growth of organizations and people. The reality is that I have taken these same differences which could have held me back in life and used them, used the backward way I often think, to find successful solutions to business problems that other people would never had discovered. I firmly believe that this potential for a fulfilled life is available to all children with learning differences when they learn how best to cope with the academic, social and professional challenges that they will face.

When I speak to children and their parents and teachers I offer my story and experiences as learning tools. I want them to know that through their attitudes and willingness to acknowledge and understand these differences, they too have the mechanisms available to achieve more than they ever thought possible.

Sometimes There Is Misery

The first step in the process is to understand that people with learning differences are confronted on a daily basis with situations and struggles that can create intense misery. The simplest reading assignment, presentation or conversation can create the most frustrating experiences and drive down a person's self worth, day after day. Misery was when I was in the third reading group at school and hated to be branded stupid. Misery was when I was singing in church as a child. I loved to sing and sang loudly. Only, when I saw the words, "GOD," I sang at the top of my voice, "DOG." I was ridiculed, isolated, admonished by the adults. Yet, I was fortunate that the minister of this church began to suspect that I was not some kind of rude kid, and that there was something else going on with me.

In the 1950s there was no name or recognition for how I viewed the world. However, this minister turned around his thinking; he did not see me as stupid, so he began to turn around me. He spent the time helping me, rehearsing me, preparing me, and it worked. I joined the choir and loved it. More importantly, it opened the door to one of the most critical aspects of a life with learning differences: acceptance.

People with learning differences need acceptance, not only from themselves. They also need it from their parents, teachers and friends whose support they need to succeed. Although acceptance appears an easy concept to understand, often it is one of the most formidable barriers to achieving a turning point in life for a child with differences. Without internal and external acceptance, this child will not be open to develop the coping mechanisms that are right for him or her. The minister opened that window of acceptance for me and all parents and teachers must understand its power as well.

Denial, however is an equally powerful psychological tool and I have seen too many parents who wrap themselves up in the comfort of denial. It happens around the first or second grade for children with learning differences. How could it happen to their children, who look so normal? They want to help, and yet they deny the severity of the problem and deny that it will remain for their child's entire life. Or I encounter many teachers who will not recognize the severity, thinking that some special classes are adequate, and they are geared to just pushing the kids along. I know. In my case, I kept on being pushed along, being miserable at every stage and not making progress. This denial continues right through to college. These institutions may say that they accept students with learning differences. I have found that often the day to day acceptance of this fact is missing and there are limited support mechanisms to help them achieve success. From first grade teachers to university professors, there is often limited understanding that people with learning differences do not think in a linear fashion. Without this knowledge, educators are ill equipped to provide the support that is necessary.

Moving On and Compensating

Thus the second step in the process is to accept these differences fully, work to understand the complete ramifications of these differences and devise the right compensation methods that can create turning points in children's lives. The key to this acceptance is the full knowledge that we will need support and coping mechanisms for the rest of our lives.

When I began to make my way in the corporate, financial world, working for prestigious institutions with brilliant well-educated people, there were countless times that I was afflicted with high anxiety and intense insecurity from my inability to concentrate on one subject at a time. My coping mechanism for this anxiety is a simple one—a mirror. When I am on the phone, I look in the mirror, make eye contact with myself, so that I can concentrate on the conversation. It works. At times now, I look at myself on a video screen to help me concentrate and stay focused. I eliminate the misery of being out of control, by accepting that this is a part of me and designing a solution that works. Another problem that can put me into misery is that I have difficulty concentrating when I read. By accepting that problem, knowing it will always be with me I devised a solution that enables me to focus. Whenever I get a distracting thought, I stop reading and speak this thought into a tape recorder. By the fifth time, I am able to concentrate on the subject, having put my distracting thoughts into another place.

What is interesting is that the many coping mechanisms that I use not only help me cope with the daily aspects of life, they also have helped to create unusual solutions to business problems that evade others. Because people with differences think more. First we think about something and then we think about our thinking. Our brains may be exercised more than most. In order for me to begin the workday, I ready my mind for thinking. My day starts at 3:00 AM in the morning. I wake up that early to practice reading and comprehension. I do very simple math problems; I meditate. I relax. This reduces a level of high anxiety that I and others with learning differences face every day of our lives when we are placed in challenging positions. It also does something else; it relaxes my mind so that the many different thoughts and associations racing through my brain can be pulled together to come up with unconventional and extremely successful ideas for the companies with which I have worked.

An Unconventional Approach to Business

People with learning differences naturally question things that other people do not. Because I question why letters look a certain way or question why my thoughts can be so disconnected at times, this questioning leads me to question other things that people take for granted. For example when I was first hired by Citibank to work with their five billion dollar branch in Greece, I found that customers complained of poor service and the bank was losing money. I questioned something conventional. Why was the bank president sitting in his executive office so far away from the customers? So I put his desk in the middle of the lobby so he could hear and see the problems first hand. This little move resulted in a complete overhaul of the consumer bank and the installation of new technology. New accounts started to pour in and the bank profits rose 5,000 percent in less than five years. There are many other examples where my seemingly backward look of the world led to solutions that were unique and successful. It all comes down to acceptance that we are different and the motivation to develop individual ways to compensate.

We are also fortunate that we have the technology now to assist us and to reduce the frustration of daily tasks. Five hundred different numbers are programmed into my cell phone so that I do not have to deal with the difficulty of wrong numbers. My laptop and computer keep my schedule and organize my work. When I give a speech, I use special Tele-

Prompters, with for example, question marks at the beginning of sentences not at the end and a little listening device in my ear, so that my assistant can prompt me if I forget words or get distracted. The point is that we should continually look for new ways to harness technology to help compensate for the daily struggles that impede finding our talents. Technology for us does not only mean a faster foundation of information, it means a foundation of secure information on which we can relax enough to discover the talents we have to offer, not just the obstacles we have to face.

Educators and parents must work aggressively to ensure that these types of solutions are available to their children. We cannot deny the fact that we are different. It is not just a matter of being slow in reading or having trouble at school. Dyslexia can effect every single aspect of a person's life—both personal and professional. It can railroad self-esteem, undermine confidence, isolate and intimidate. And, yet, I know that does not have to be the case.

Support and Understanding Creates Hope

It takes courage and strength to shed the limitations of the different box that frames our reality. It is essential to have the support of parents, advocates, friends and teachers who take nothing for granted about a person with learning differences. This support and understanding builds a level of acceptance that will create the mechanisms needed to compensate for the differences.

It will also create hope.

When I was talking recently to a group of children with learning differences, one girl raised her hand and said, "My parents said that I will never go to college. I have to go to a trade school," and she starts crying. I said, "No, that does not have to be the case." And she said, "But I have to go to trade school." I said, "In my world, the word 'but' is not in my vocabulary. How about using and thinking the word 'and?' I went to trade school first and then I went to college."

This simple change created a noticeable shift in her thinking. I could see it in seconds as the expression across her face changed to one of hope. When someone tells me that she cannot do something, I make her say, "up until now." Once this change occurs, the potential for creativity, unique contributions to society and for personal happiness grows as well.

I do not pretend to know all the answers or can solve all the problems that learning different people confront. I do know, however, that sharing information, new resources and new ideas and promoting continual efforts to educate teachers and parents can result in true success.

Organizations to Contact

The editors have compiled the following list of organizations concerned with the issues debated in this book. The descriptions are derived from materials provided by the organizations. All have publications or information available for interested readers. The list was compiled on the date of publication of the present volume; the information provided here may change. Be aware that many organizations take several weeks or longer to respond to inquiries, so allow as much time as possible.

Association on Higher Education and Disability (AHEAD)
107 Commerce Center Drive, Suite 204
Huntersville, NC   28078
(704) 947-7779 • fax: (704)-948-7779
e-mail: ahead@ahead.org
Web site: www.ahead.org

An international professional association, the Association on Higher Education and Disability (AHEAD) is committed to helping individuals with learning disabilities participate fully in postsecondary education. Founded in 1977, AHEAD trains higher education personnel through workshops, publications, and consultation. Members are professionals who raise awareness of disability issues on campuses. AHEAD publishes the *Journal of Postsecondary Education and Disabilities* and the e-newsletter *ALERT*.

Attention Deficit Disorder Association (ADDA)
15000 Commerce Parkway, Suite C, Mount Laurel, NJ   08054
(856) 439-9099 • fax: (856) 439-0525
Web site: www.add.org

A nonprofit organization founded in 1989, the Attention Deficit Disorder Association (ADDA) provides information, resources, and networking for adults with attention deficit disorder and for the professionals who work with them. The goal of ADDA is to reflect both the scientific perspective and human experiences so that there can be proper diagnosis, treatment, and guidance for those with attention deficit disorder. This organization holds an annual national conference and offers teleclasses as well as audio, video, and written source materials. It publishes the journal *FOCUS* and the e-newsletter *ADDA eNews.*

Children and Adults with Attention Deficit Hyperactivity Disorder (CHADD)
8181 Professional Place, Suite 150, Landover, MD   20785
(301) 306-7070 • fax: (301) 306-7090
Web site: www.chadd.org

With two hundred local chapters, Children and Adults with Attention Deficit Hyperactivity Disorder (CHADD) is a major nonprofit organization for attention deficit disorder, offering information and assistance to individuals and their families nationwide. Begun in 1987 to address the frustration and feelings of isolation experienced by the parents of children with attention deficit disorder, the organization has grown to serve people of all ages with the disability. It publishes the journal *Attention!*

The Council for Learning Disabilities (CLD)
11184 Antioch Road, Overland Park, KS   66210
(913) 491-1011 • fax: (913) 491-1012
e-mail: lnease@cldinternational.org
Web site: www.cldinternational.org

An international organization in existence for more than twenty years, the Council for Learning Disabilities (CLD) focuses on helping students with learning disabilities. Its research committee sponsors an annual panel on the "must reads" for educators, and local chapters hold local and regional activities to share current information about learning disabilities as well as offering a network for professionals. CLD publishes three journals: *Learning Disability Quarterly, LD Forum,* and *Intervention in School and Clinic.*

Foundation for People with Learning Disabilities (FPLD)
Ninth Floor Sea Containers House   SEI 9QB
  London
(020) 7803 1100 • fax: (020) 7803 1111
e-mail: fpld@fpld.org.uk
Web site: www.learningdisabilities.org.uk

Part of the Mental Health Foundation, with offices in London and Glasgow, the Foundation for People with Learning Disabilities (FPLD) promotes rights, a better quality of life, and opportunities for those with learning disabilities. It works on spreading knowledge and information, making practical changes in services for those with learning disabilities, and promoting research and development of projects that help them. The FPLD publishes the journal *Foundation Stones*.

HEATH Resource Center
2134 G Street NW, Washington, DC   20052
(202) 973-0904 • fax: (202) 994-3365
e-mail: askheath@gwu.edu
Web site: www.heath.gwu.edu

The HEATH Resource Center is affiliated with the George Washington University Graduate School of Education and Human Development. It is an online clearinghouse of information about postsecondary education for individuals with disabilities. Founded in 1984, it was acquired by George Washington University in 2001 to respond to inquiries and to gather and disseminate information. It shares data about support systems, policies, and opportunities at American campuses and other postsecondary training and educational entities. The center publishes the newsletter *Information from HEATH*.

The International Dyslexia Association (IDA)
40 York Road, Fourth Floor, Baltimore, MD   21204
(410) 296-0232 • fax: (410) 321-5069
Web site: www.interdys.org

The oldest learning disability organization in the nation, the International Dyslexia Association (IDA) was founded in 1949 in memory of Dr. Samuel T. Orton, the neurologist who was one of the first to identify dyslexia. IDA is devoted to the study and treatment of dyslexia through local branches as well as partners in many other countries. It offers conferences and support groups through many of its more than forty local branches, and some IDA branches also offer testing, tutoring, and related assistance. The organization holds an annual international conference with over two hundred experts in the field. It also funds research and advocates for legal rights for the dyslexic. IDA publishes *Perspectives Newsletter* and the journal *Annals of Dyslexia*.

Learning Disabilities Association of America (LDA)
4156 Library Road, Pittsburgh, PA 15234
(412) 341-1515 • fax: (412) 344-0224
Web site: www.ldaamerica.org

In 1963 parents of children with learning disabilities held a national conference in Chicago and, the next year, formed the Association for Children with Learning Disabilities, which later became the Learning Disabilities Association of America (LDA). With two hundred state and local affiliates, it is the largest nonprofit volunteer organization advocating for individuals with learning disabilities. The international membership covers twenty-seven countries with over fifteen thousand members. LDA hopes to reduce the incidence of learning disabilities and to help understanding and treatment in communities throughout the world. LDA publishes *Learning Disabilities: A Multidisciplinary Journal*.

Learning Disabilities Worldwide (LDW)
PO Box 142, Weston, MA 02493
(781) 890-5399 • fax: (781) 890-0555
e-mail: info@ldworldwide.org
Web site: www.ldworldwide.org

In 1965 the Learning Disabilities Association of Massachusetts (LDAM) was created to support parents of children with learning disabilities. It began to publish materials to help parents, educators and medical professionals work together. Written by experts in the field, these publications became known internationally. In 2004 LDAM became Learning Disabilities Worldwide (LDW), an international organization devoted to publishing and dispersing the latest information about learning disabilities. LDW publishes two journals: *Learning Disabilities; A Contemporary Journal* and *Insights on Learning Disabilities: From Prevailing Theories to Validated Practices.*

The National Association for the Education of African American Children with Learning Disabilities (NAEAACLD)
PO Box 09521, Columbus, OH 43209
(614) 237-6021
e-mail: info@aacld.org
Web site: www.charityadvantage.com/aacld

The National Association for the Education of African American Children with Learning Disabilities (NAEAACLD), founded in 1999, focuses on the special issues facing African American children with learning disabilities. Its Web site states: "The organization's mission is to link information and resources provided by an established network of individuals and organizations experienced in minority research and special education with parents, educators, and others responsible for providing a quality education for all students." NAEAACLD believes that any program that is put in place to help African American children will assist all children.

National Center for Gender Issues and ADHD (NCGIADD)
3268 Arcadia Place NW, Washington, DC 20015
(888) 238-8588 • fax: (202) 966-1561
e-mail: contact@ncgiadd.org
Web site: www.ncgiadd.org

Devoted to the understanding of girls and women with attention deficit hyperactivity disorder, the National Center for Gender Issues and ADHD (NCGIADD) was founded by Patricia Quinn, MD and Kathleen Nadeau, PhD to promote awareness, advocacy, and research about females with the disorder. The organization disseminates information through their Web site, as well as seminars, a newsletter and a magazine, press releases, and publications. It also sponsors programs and videos to document the struggles of women and girls with attention deficit disorder. NCGIADD publishes the e-newsletter *ADvance On-line* and the journal *ADDvance.*

National Center for Learning Disabilities (NCLD)

381 Park Avenue South, Suite 1401, New York, NY   10016
(212) 545-7510 • fax: (212) 545-9665
e-mail: help@ncld.org
Web site: www.ncld.org

Begun in 1977 by Pete and Carrie Rozelle as the Foundation for Children with Learning Disabilities, the National Center for Learning Disabilities (NCLD) expanded its scope in 1989, at which time Anne Ford assumed the role as chairman of the board and led the organization for twelve years. The NCLD believes its role is ensuring that the 15 million American adolescents and adults with learning disabilities have opportunities to succeed in school, work, and life. NCLD publishes the e-newsletter *LD News.*

National Dissemination Center for Children and Youth with Disabilities (NICHCY)

PO Box 1492, Washington, DC   20013
(202) 884-8200 • fax: (202) 884-8441
e-mail: nichcy@aed.org
Web site: www.nichcy.org

The National Dissemination Center for Children and Youth with Disabilities (NICHCY) specializes in offering information on learning disabilities and programs, as well as the Individuals with Disabilities Act and the No Child Left Behind Act. Its special focus is children and young adults from birth to twenty-two years of age. It offers a bilingual Web site and toll-free number where questions and concerns are addressed in both Spanish and English. There is an interactive link for children called Zigawhat!

Schwab Foundation for Learning

1650 South Amphlett Boulevard, Suite 300
San Mateo, CA   94402
(650) 655-2410 • fax: (650) 655-2411
Web site: www.schwablearning.org

Founded in 1989, the Schwab Foundation for Learning grew out of Charles Schwab's struggle with dyslexia and out of the frustration he and his wife had trying to get help for their dyslexic son. Funded by the Charles and Helen Schwab Foundation, the organization tries to help parents, teachers, and other professionals obtain information to aid students with learning disabilities by offering resources through its Web site, publications, programs, and educational partnerships. The Schwab Foundation for Learning has a Web site specifically for children with learning disabilities called www.SparkTop.org with videos, activities, and graphics. The organization also publishes the e-newsletter *SchwabLearning.org*.

Smart Kids with Learning Disabilities

PO Box 2726, Westport, CT   06880
(203) 226-6831 • fax: (203) 226-4861
Web site: www.smartkidswithld.org

With the goal of empowering parents and changing the negative perception of learning disabilities, the nonprofit Smart Kids with Learning Disabilities was established in 2000 to offer "action-oriented" information through its newsletter, Web site, and educational programs. It sponsors the annual Smart Kids Youth Achievement Award given to an individual for demonstrating outstanding accomplishments or service to others. A winner is selected from candidates nominated by the public. The organization publishes the newsletter *Smart Kids*.

For Further Reading

Books

Lenard Adler and Mari Florence, *Scattered Minds: Hope and Help for Adults with Attention Deficit Hyperactivity Disorder*. New York: Putnam, 2006.

R.A. Barkley, *Attention-Deficit Hyperactivity Disorder: A Handbook for Diagnosis and Treatment*. New York: Guilford Press, 1990.

Regina Cicci, *What's Wrong with Me?: Learning Disabilities at Home and School*. Baltimore: York Press, 1995.

Joyanne Cobb, *Learning How to Learn: Getting to and Surviving College When You Have a Learning Disability*, rev. ed. Arlington, VA: Child & Family Press, 2003.

Roslyn Dolber, *College and Career Success for Students with Learning Disabilities*. Chicago: VGM Career Horizons, 1996.

Mavis L. Donahue and Bernice Y.L. Wong, eds., *The Social Dimensions of Learning Disabilities: Essays in Honor of Tanis Bryan*. Florence, KY: LEA, 2002.

Paul J. Gerber and Henry B. Reiff, *Speaking for Themselves: Ethnographic Interviews with Adults with Learning Disabilities*. Ann Arbor: University of Michigan Press, 1991.

Edward M. Hallowell and John J. Ratey, *Answers to Distraction*. New York: Pantheon, 1994.

Edward M. Hallowell and John J. Ratey, *Delivered from Distraction: Getting the Most Out of Life with Attention Deficit Disorder*. New York: Ballantine, 2005.

Edward M. Hallowell and John J. Ratey, *Driven to Distraction: Recognizing and Coping with Attention Deficit Disorder from Childhood Through Adulthood*. New York: Touchstone, 1995.

Thom Hartmann, *Attention Deficit Disorder: A Different Perspective*. Grass Valley, CA: Underwood, 1997.

Bruce Jenner, *Finding the Champion Within: A Step-by-Step Plan for Reaching Your Full Potential*. New York: Fireside, 1999.

Kate Kelly and Peggy Ramundo, *You Mean I'm Not Lazy, Stupid or Crazy?!: The Classic Self-Help Book for Adults with Attention Deficit Disorder*. New York: Scribner, 2006.

Kate Kelly, Peggy Ramundo, and D. Steven Ledingham, *The ADDed Dimension: Everyday Advice for Adults with ADD*. New York: Scribner, 1997.

Richard Lavoie, *It's So Much Work to Be Your Friend: Helping the Child with Learning Disabilities Find Social Success*. New York: Touchstone, 2005.

Nancy Lelewer, *Something's Not Right: One Family's Struggle with Learning Disabilities*. Acton, MA: Vander-Wyk & Burnham, 1994.

Jonathan Mooney and David Cole, *Learning Outside the Lines: Two Ivy League Students with Learning Disabilities and ADHD Give You the Tools for Academic Success and Educational Revolution*. New York: Fireside, 2000.

Kathleen G. Nadeau, *Help4ADD@High School*. Bethesda, MD: Advantage Books, 1998.

Kathleen G. Nadeau and Patricia O. Quinn, *Understanding Women with AD/HD*. Silver Spring, MD: Advantage Books, 2002.

Penny Hutchins Paquette and Cheryl Gerson Tuttle, *Learning Disabilities: The Ultimate Teen Guide*. Lanham, MD: Scarecrow Press, 2003.

Thomas W. Phelan, *All About Attention Deficit Disorder*, 2nd ed. Glen Ellyn, IL: Child Management, 2000.

Patricia O. Quinn, *ADD and the College Student: A Guide for High School and College Students with Attention Deficit Disorder*, rev. ed. Washington, DC: Magination Press, 2001.

Margaret Byrd Rawson, *The Many Faces of Dyslexia*. Baltimore: International Dyslexia Association, 1996.

Regina G. Richards, *The Writing Dilemma: Understanding Dysgraphia*. Riverside, CA: Richards Therapy Center, 1998.

Joan Shapiro and Rebecca Rich, *Facing Learning Disabilities in the Adult Years*. New York: Oxford University Press, 1999.

Juliana M. Taymans, Lynda L. West, and Madeline Sullivan, eds., *Unlocking Potential: College and Other Choices for People with LD and AD/HD*. Bethesda, MD: Woodbine House, 2000.

S.A. Vogel and P.B. Adelman, *Success for College Students with Learning Disabilities*. New York: Springer-Verlag, 1992.

Beth Walker, *The Girls' Guide to AD/HD: Don't Lose This Book!* Bethesda, MD: Woodbine House, 2004.

Thomas G. West, *In the Mind's Eye: Visual Thinkers, Gifted People with Dyslexia and Other Learning Difficulties, Computer Images and the Ironies of Creativity*. Buffalo, NY: Prometheus, 1997.

Periodicals

G. Bialock and J.R. Patton, "Transition and Students with Learning Disabilities: Creating Sound Futures," *Journal of Learning Disabilities* 29, no. 1 (1996).

A. Burka, "The Emotional Reality of a Learning Disability," *Annals of Dyslexia* 33 (1983).

Diane Connell, "The Invisible Disability," *Instructor Magazine*, September 2003.

Erin A. Fetzer, "The Gifted/Learning-Disabled Child: A Guide for Teachers and Parents," *Gifted Child Today*, July 2000.

Thom Gillespie, "LOL: Lots of Luck? Laughing Out Loud? Or Learning Outside the Lines?" *Technos: Quarterly for Education and Technology*, Winter 2000.

Christine Gorman, "The New Science of Dyslexia," *Time*, July 28, 2003.

Barbara Kantrowitz and Anne Underwood, "Dyslexia and the New Science of Reading," *Newsweek*, November 22, 1999.

Lucy M. Lockly, "Paying Attention to Attention-Deficit Disorders," *Library Journal*, January 1999.

David L. Marcus, "What Do You Do If School Is a Struggle?" *U.S. News & World Report*, September 11, 2000.

Ann Marsh, "When the Alphabet Is a Struggle," *Forbes*, September 1999.

Betsy Morris, "Overcoming Dyslexia," *Fortune*, May 13, 2002.

John O'Neil, "A Clearer Path to Reading Fluency," *New York Times*, April 27, 2004.

Abbie Rabine, "I'm Not Stupid!" *Campus Life*, July 2001.

Jeannie Ralston, "Could Your Child Have a Learning Disability? And What Should You Do If She Does?" *Family Life*, March 1, 2001.

Carl Sherman, "The Dangers of Self-Medication," *ADDitude*, February–March 2007.

S. Shaywitz, "Dyslexia," *Scientific American* 275 (1996).

L.S. Siegel, "The IQ Is Irrelevant to the Definition of Learning Disabilities," *Journal of Learning Disabilities*, May 1990.

Pat Wingert and Barbara Kantrowitz, "Why Andy Couldn't Read," *Newsweek*, October 27, 1997.

Terri Yablonsky, Stat "Program Helps Kids Sharpen Their Memory," *Chicago Tribune*, May 22, 2007.

Eileen Zimmerman, "On the Job, Learning Disabilities Can Often Hide in Plain Sight," *New York Times*, December 17, 2006.

Index